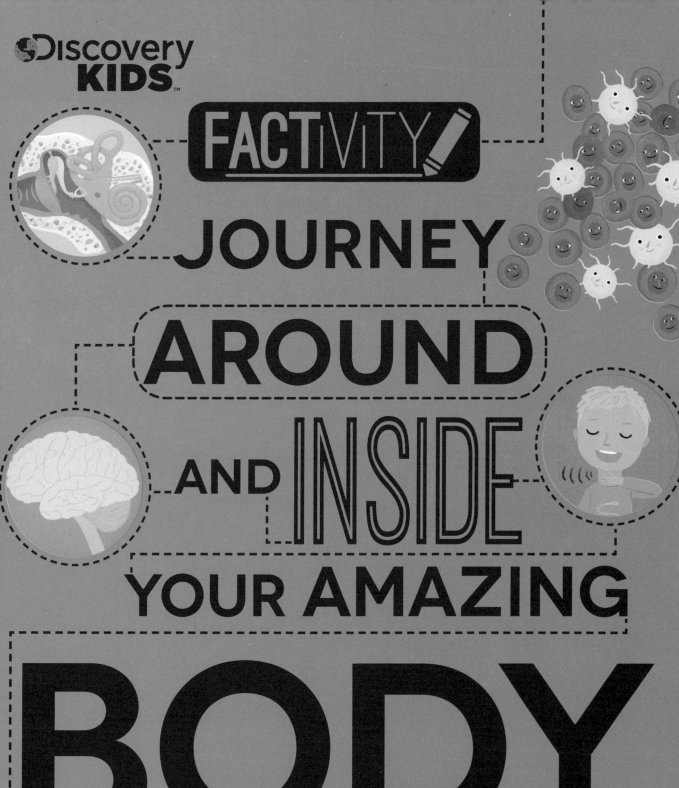

FACTIVITY

JOURNEY AROUND AND INSIDE YOUR AMAZING BODY

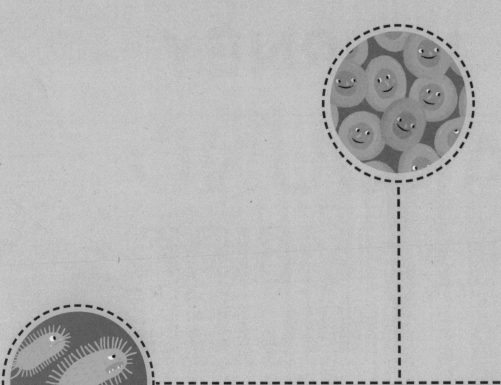

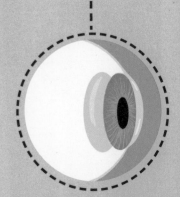

This edition published by Parragon Books Ltd in 2014 and distributed by
Parragon Inc.
440 Park Avenue South, 13th Floor
New York, NY 10016
www.parragon.com

Written by Anna Claybourne
Illustrated by Mar Ferrero
Consultant: Dr Clare J. Ray

ISBN 978-1-4723-5780-9

Printed in China

Discovery KIDS™

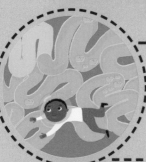

FACTIVITY!

JOURNEY

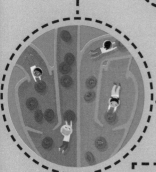

AROUND

AND INSIDE

YOUR AMAZING

BODY

PaRragon

Bath • New York • Cologne • Melbourne • Delhi
Hong Kong • Shenzhen • Singapore • Amsterdam

Contents

Your amazing human body

Your body is an incredible living, breathing, moving, eating, talking, thinking machine. Look closer and you'll discover that your body has many different parts, all working together.

> Everybody has a body!

> We may look different, but we're all human.

> Every body is amazing!

> Look around and see how different our bodies look.

HUNDREDS of bones and muscles.

THOUSANDS of miles of tiny tubes.

MILLIONS of hairs.

Just ONE human body has...

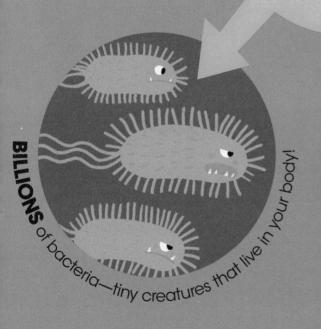

BILLIONS of bacteria—tiny creatures that live in your body!

TRILLIONS of cells—the tiny building blocks that make up living things.

Being human

Living things come in all shapes and sizes, but human beings are unlike most other creatures. We walk upright on two legs, we use our brains to think and our hands to make and do useful things.

The human body is pretty smart when you think about all the things it does.

- Your body grows bigger and bigger until you're an adult.
- It builds new body parts to replace old ones.
- It repairs itself if it gets broken.
- It has special body parts to sense light, sounds, smells, tastes, and objects.

My pet dog walks on four legs and has paws instead of hands with fingers and a thumb.

Your body even reads books about itself!

When you look at other animals, you can see what makes humans different.

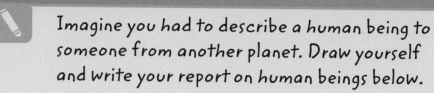

Imagine you had to describe a human being to someone from another planet. Draw yourself and write your report on human beings below.

HUMAN BEING

Size ....

Appearance ....

Color ....

Body parts ....

Senses ....

Skills ....

....

Body map

This handy body map will help you as you explore the human body.

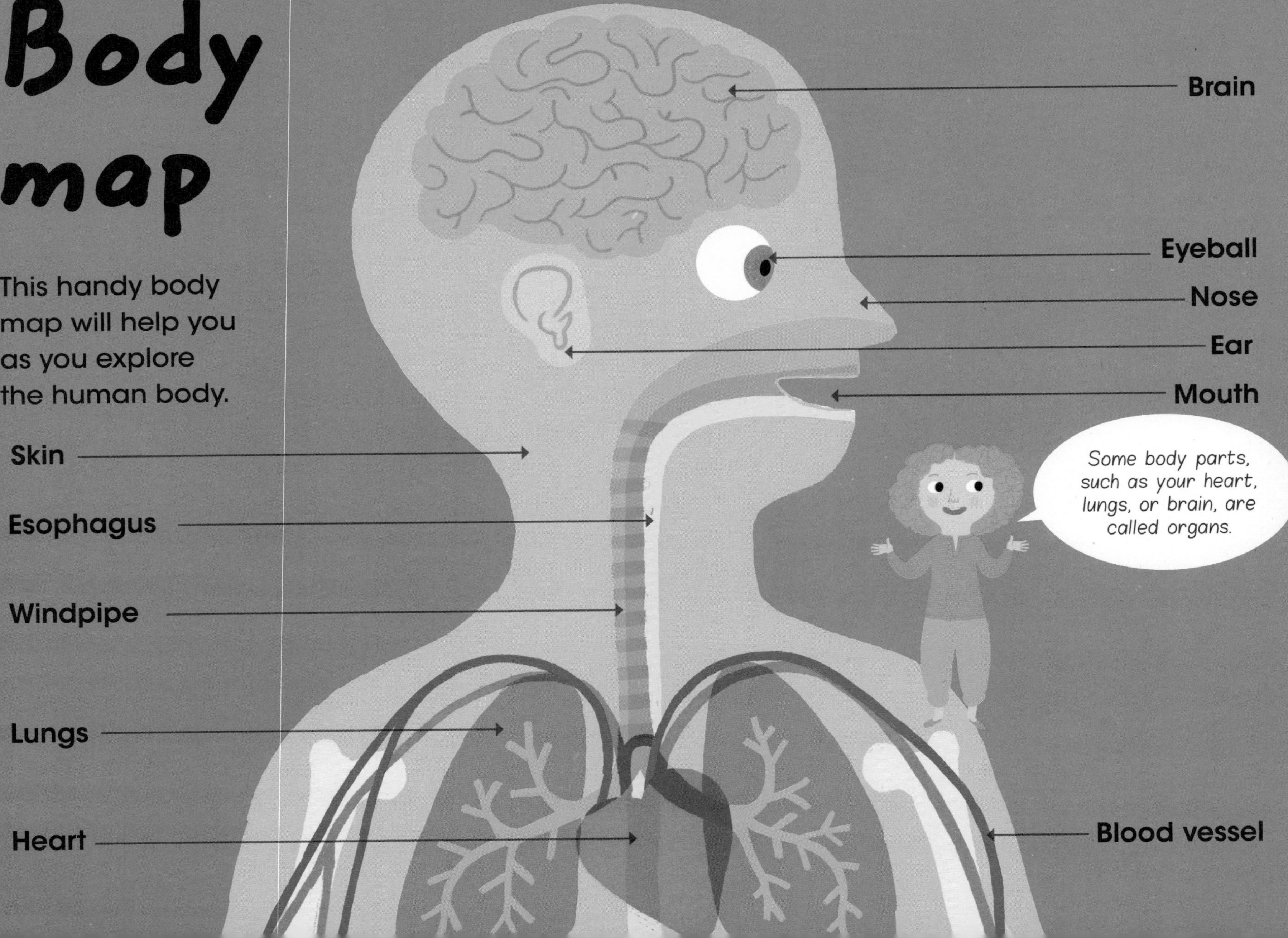

Brain

Eyeball

Nose

Ear

Mouth

Some body parts, such as your heart, lungs, or brain, are called organs.

Skin

Esophagus

Windpipe

Lungs

Heart

Blood vessel

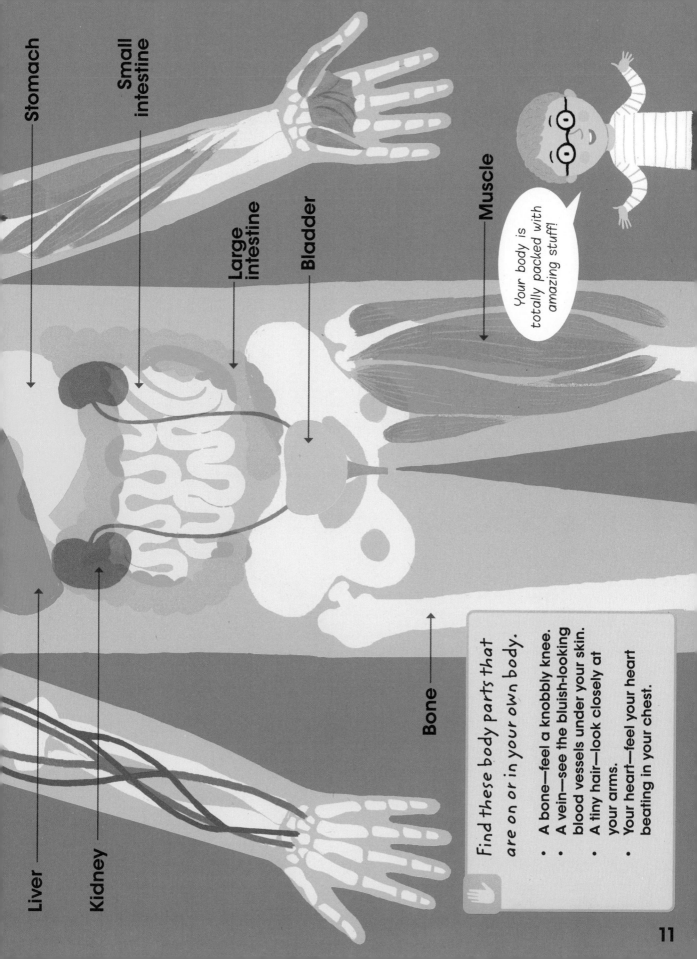

Stomach

Small intestine

Large intestine

Bladder

Muscle

Your body is totally packed with amazing stuff!

Liver

Kidney

Bone

Find these body parts that are on or in your own body.

- A bone—feel a knobbly knee.
- A vein—see the bluish-looking blood vessels under your skin.
- A tiny hair—look closely at your arms.
- Your heart—feel your heart beating in your chest.

It all starts with cells

Cells are the tiny building blocks that the body is made of. They work hard all the time, keeping your body moving, breathing, and alive.

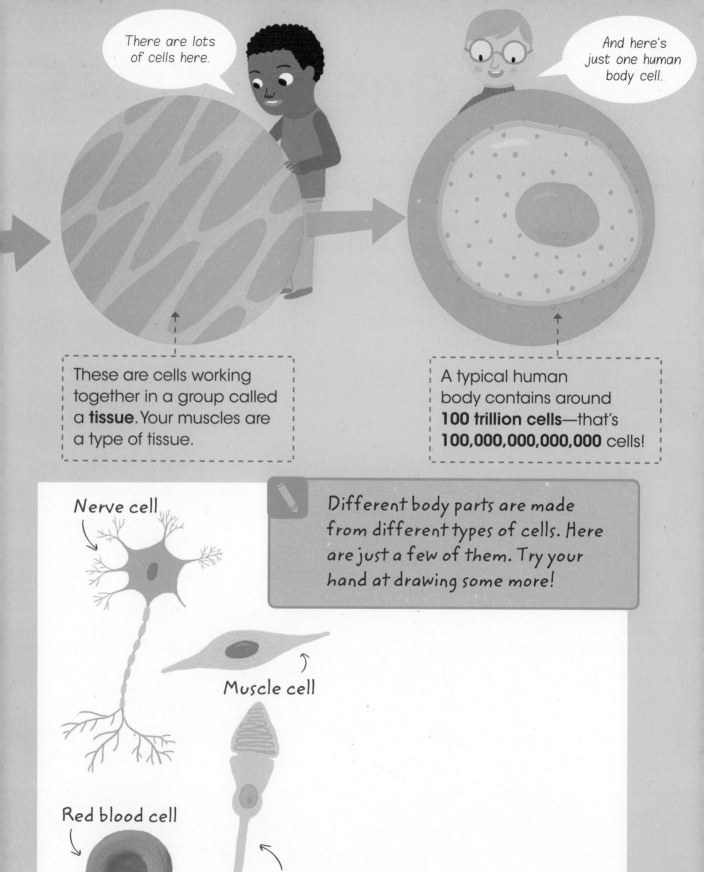

There are lots of cells here.

And here's just one human body cell.

These are cells working together in a group called a **tissue**. Your muscles are a type of tissue.

A typical human body contains around **100 trillion cells**—that's **100,000,000,000,000** cells!

Different body parts are made from different types of cells. Here are just a few of them. Try your hand at drawing some more!

Nerve cell

Muscle cell

Red blood cell

Light sensor cell

Bones and muscles

Bones give your body its shape and allow you to move.
Your skeleton has more than 200 bones. Muscles are joined
to your bones, and you use them every time you move.

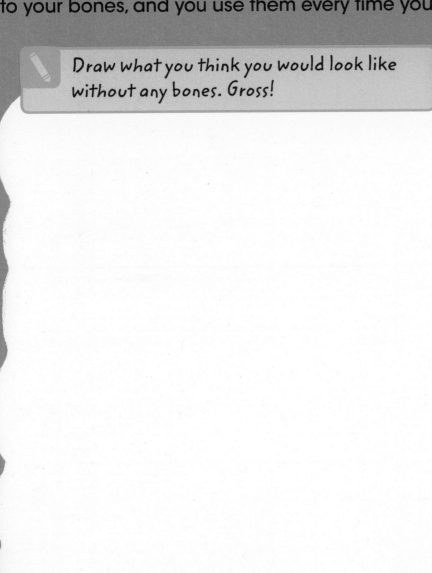

Draw what you think you would look like without any bones. Gross!

Hey!
Are we
related?

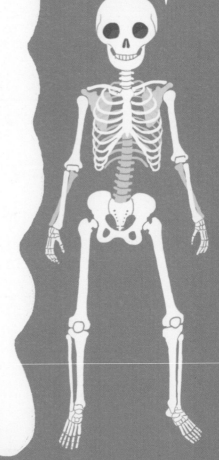

Without me, you'd be a helpless, wobbly blob!

Bones are your body's framework. Your leg bones are thick and strong to hold your body's weight.

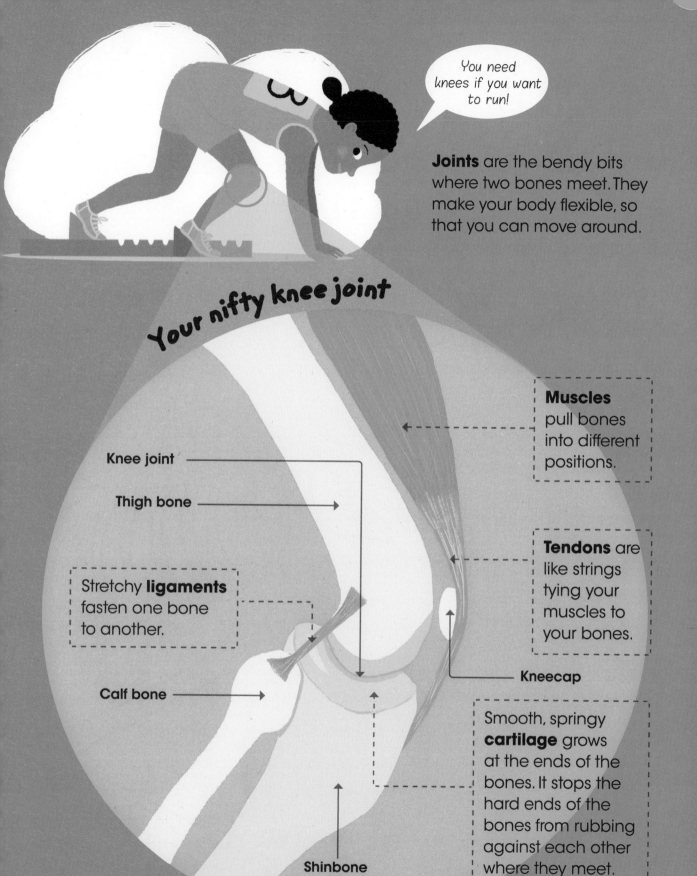

You need knees if you want to run!

Joints are the bendy bits where two bones meet. They make your body flexible, so that you can move around.

Your nifty knee joint

Muscles pull bones into different positions.

Knee joint

Thigh bone

Tendons are like strings tying your muscles to your bones.

Stretchy **ligaments** fasten one bone to another.

Calf bone

Kneecap

Smooth, springy **cartilage** grows at the ends of the bones. It stops the hard ends of the bones from rubbing against each other where they meet.

Shinbone

Your skeleton

All your bones join together to make up your skeleton. You can't see your skeleton because it's covered by skin and muscle, so take a quick peek at all those bones below!

Complete the other half of this skeleton by tracing over the faint lines. Then color it in!

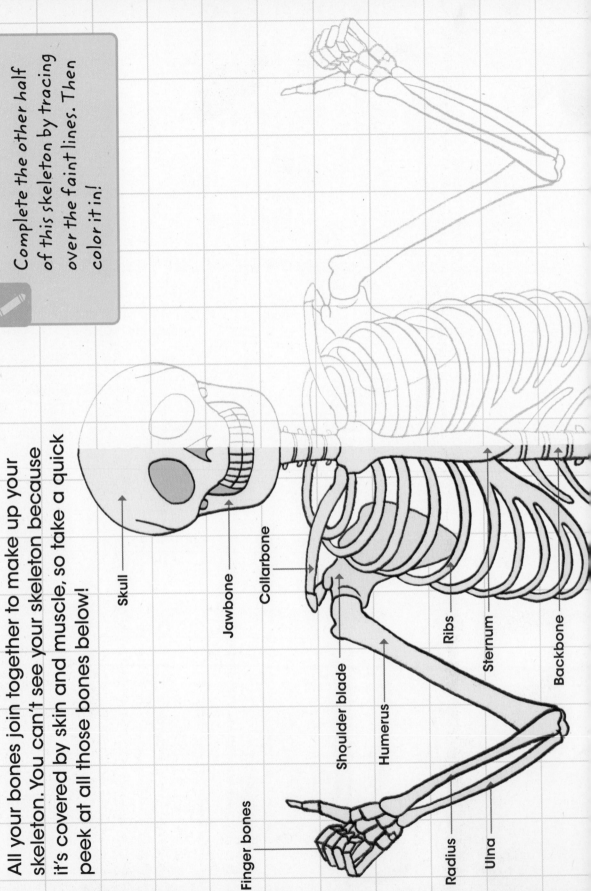

Skull

Jawbone

Collarbone

Shoulder blade

Humerus

Ribs

Sternum

Backbone

Finger bones

Radius

Ulna

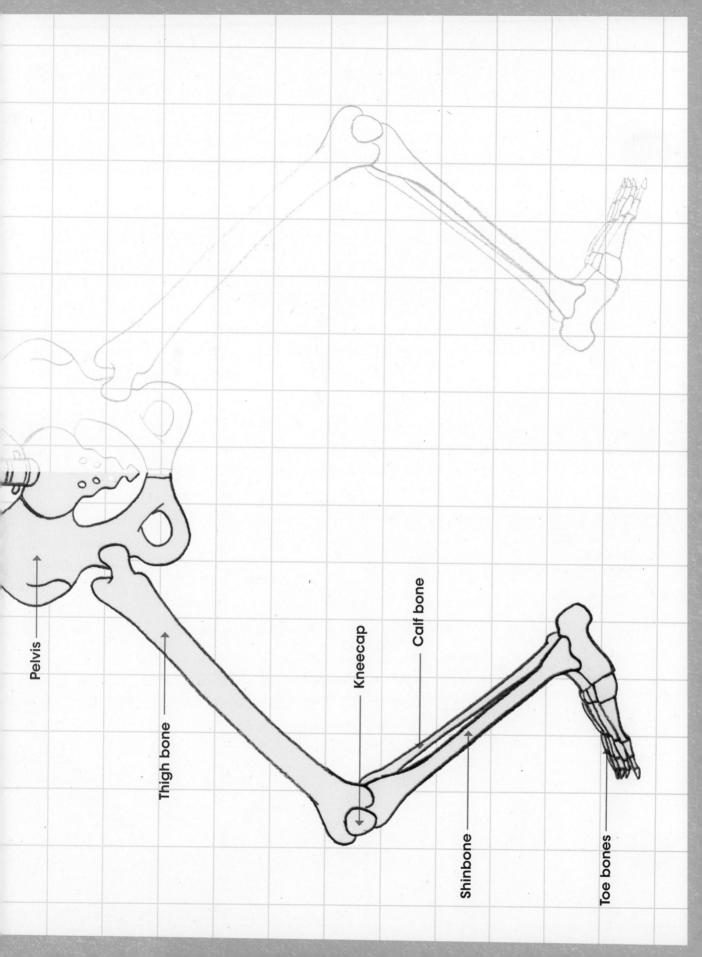

Pelvis

Thigh bone

Kneecap

Calf bone

Shinbone

Toe bones

Look inside a bone

Bones may be hard, but they aren't made of stone! They are alive, like the rest of you. Bones are made up of several layers.

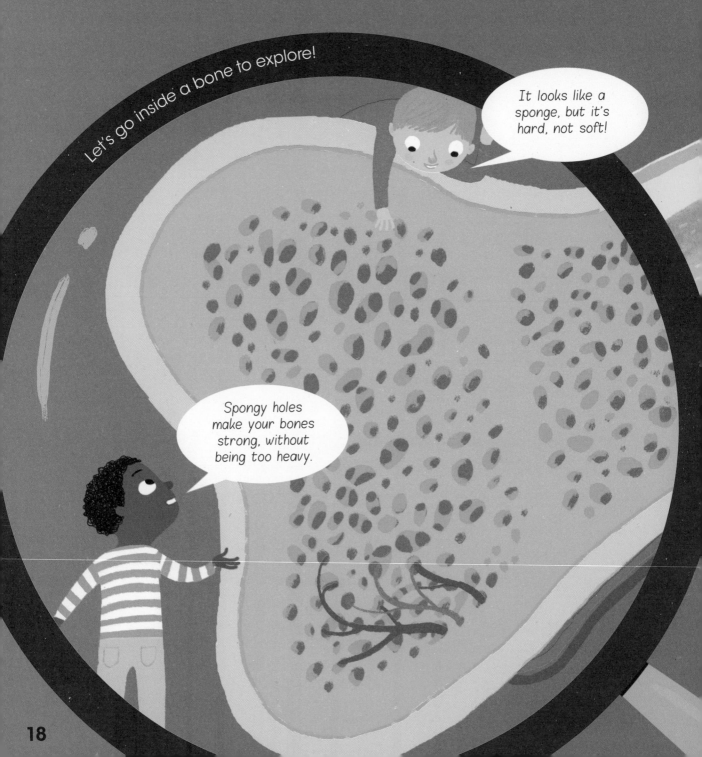

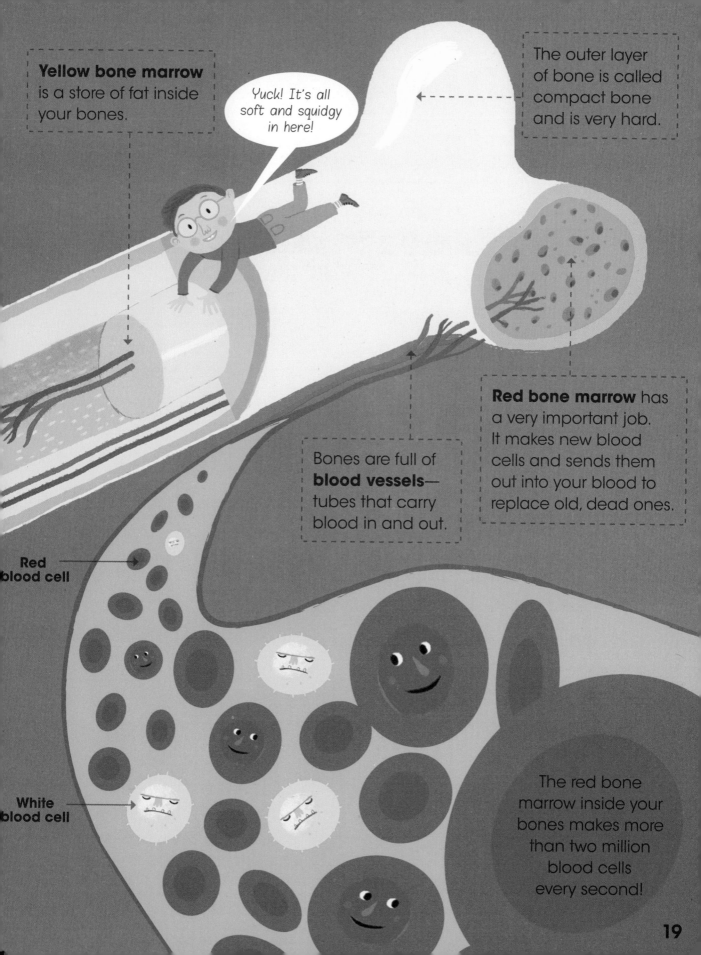

An unlucky break!

Bones are strong, but they can break or crack. If you've ever broken a bone, you'll know it really hurts. Luckily, bones can mend themselves, too!

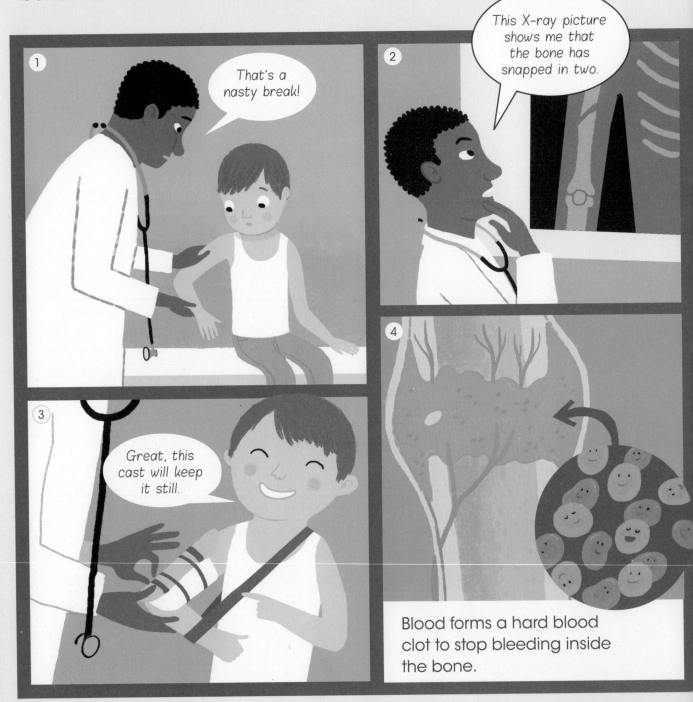

1. *That's a nasty break!*

2. *This X-ray picture shows me that the bone has snapped in two.*

3. *Great, this cast will keep it still.*

4. Blood forms a hard blood clot to stop bleeding inside the bone.

Tough, stringy strands start to fill the gap.

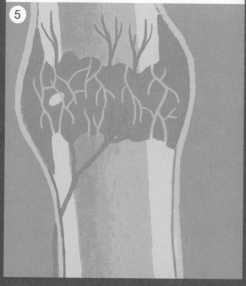

5

Bone cells build up in the gap, making a solid bone repair.

6

After about three months, the break will be completely healed!

No way!

7

Yippee!

When it's mended, your arm will be as good as new!

Color the shapes with an X in them black to create a cool X-ray picture.

Customize a cast

A broken bone is set in a cast to help it heal. It stops the patient from moving the broken bone and damaging it further. It also keeps it in the right position, so that it will heal straight.

A cast can be totally annoying, but at least you can customize it. Add signatures, doodle some designs, or add cartoon pictures to make this cast the coolest.

Muscle power!

Muscles work by *pulling*. Loads of tiny muscle cells work together to make the muscle shorter. This pulls on the bone to make it move. That's teamwork!

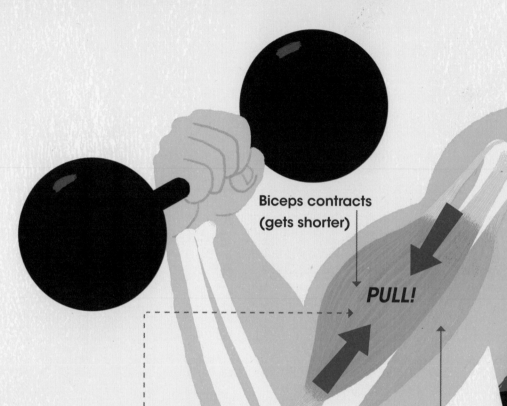

Biceps contracts
(gets shorter)

PULL!

Triceps relaxes
(gets longer)

The **biceps** is connected to two arm bones, joining them together. When the biceps muscle pulls, the arm bones move toward each other, and the arm bends.

But now what? Muscles can only pull. When the biceps isn't pulling on the arm, it relaxes and stops pulling. It can't push your forearm the other way.

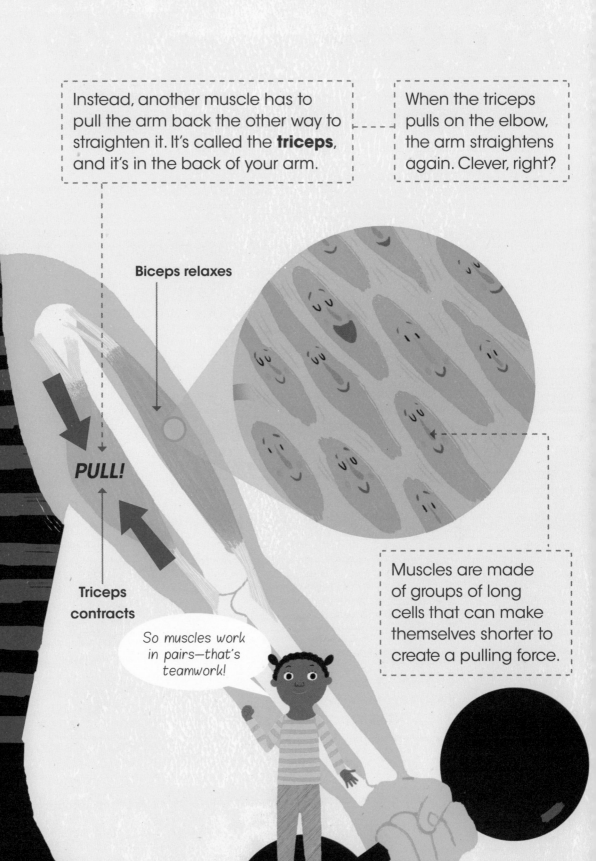

Instead, another muscle has to pull the arm back the other way to straighten it. It's called the **triceps**, and it's in the back of your arm.

When the triceps pulls on the elbow, the arm straightens again. Clever, right?

Biceps relaxes

PULL!

Triceps contracts

So muscles work in pairs—that's teamwork!

Muscles are made of groups of long cells that can make themselves shorter to create a pulling force.

25

Muscle fact zone

Muscles get your body moving, providing the power for everything from breathing and pumping blood around to running—or even just blinking!

1. Muscles are made up of millions of muscle fibers all neatly arranged in rows. Muscles make up about 40 percent of your body weight.

40%

Are you one of the few people who can use muscle power to wiggle their ears?

2. Your skeleton has about 640 different muscles to keep you on the move. You've even got muscles in your ears!

3. Even your eyes have muscles! They keep your eyes focused and control the amount of light that enters the eye. They also help you to blink.

4. Some muscles are controlled by our thoughts. Others work without us thinking about it. Your heart is made of cardiac muscle that beats automatically, 24 hours a day!

Brrr. Time to create my own heatwave!

5. Shivering uses the heat made by hundreds of muscles expanding and contracting to warm us up when it is cold.

6. The strongest muscles in your body are the muscles that you chew with. They're called the masseters!

Quick muscle quiz
How many muscles do you think your arm will use to check the correct answer to this question?

5 ⬭
25 ⬭
250 ⬭

Terrific tendons

Your fingers don't have any muscles, so how can you move them? The answer is tendons—strings that join your fingers to the muscles in your arm that make them move.

 To see how tendons work, build a model hand and make it move! Ask a grown-up to help you.

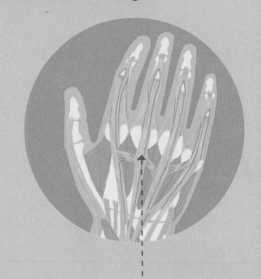

You can feel the **tendons** running along the back of your hand if you bend your fingers and then relax them. They feel a little bit like cords.

You will need:

scissors   felt-tip pen   string

tape   rubber glove   straws

❶

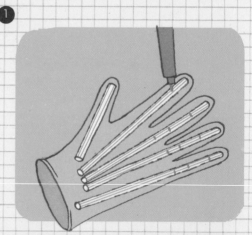

Lay the straws on the glove, and mark where the finger and thumb joints would be.

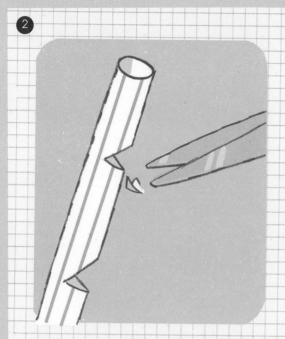

Carefully cut triangle-shaped notches at the lines in the straws to make the joints.

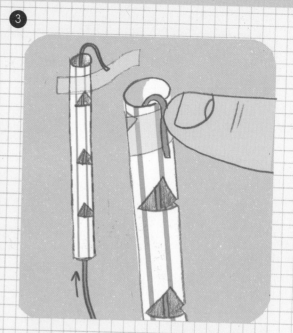

Thread strings through the straws and tape in place at the top.

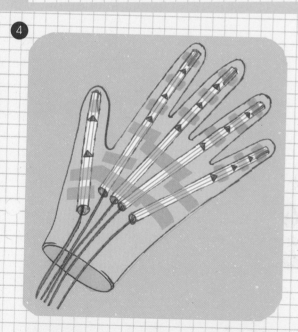

Tape the straws to the glove with the notches face up. (Don't put tape over the notches.)

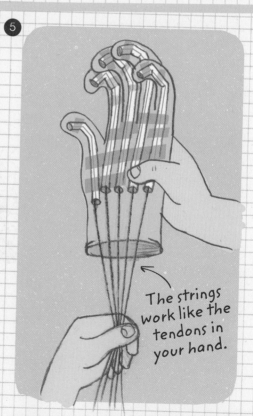

The strings work like the tendons in your hand.

Hold the glove at the wrist, and pull the strings! See how the fingers curl up on their own.

Squeezy muscles

Your body also has muscles in its organs and body tubes. Rings of muscles squeeze to move food and blood through your tubes!

FROM THE STOMACH

Let's look inside the squeezy tubes of the **small intestine!**

RELAX

SQUEEZE!

Here comes another wave of squeeziness.

Your throat muscles squeeze in the same way when you swallow.

RELAX

Rings of **muscle** squeeze in turn. The squeezing moves along the tube in waves.

The squeezing pushes the mushed food forward toward the **large intestine**.

Squeezy pump

The heart is made of muscle, too, and it also works by squeezing. It clenches tight to pump blood around your body.

Put your hand on your tummy. This is where your small intestine is.

RELAX

SQUEEZE!

Let's ride the squeezy wave!

Eeek! We're moving!

SQUEEZE!

SQUEEZE!

SQUEEZE!

RELAX

The waves of squeezing and relaxing muscles are called **peristalsis** (say: pear-i-stal-sis).

TO THE LARGE INTESTINE

Food for life

Eating food gives us the energy to live, move, and grow. It also provides the raw materials that we need to build and repair our bodies.

Figure out which groups these foods belong to. Then draw them in the gaps on the correct shelves.

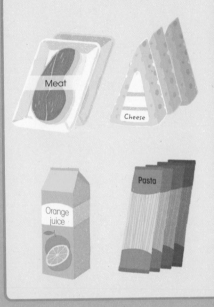

Food groups shopping list

Foods like potatoes, rice, pasta, and bread are packed with **carbohydrates** (say: car-bo-hi-drates) and provide us with energy.

Proteins help your body to grow and repair itself. Fish, meat, eggs, beans, and nuts are all rich in protein.

Fats are found in butter, cheese, and cooking oil and provide an energy store. A layer of fat under our skin keeps us warm.

Fruit, vegetables, fish, orange juice, and milk contain **vitamins** and **minerals**. They are used to make strong bones or blood cells and help our body to work.

Your blood and all your cells are mostly made of **water.** We get water from food and liquids to keep them healthy.

Foods such as cereals, fruit, and vegetables also contain fiber to keep us healthy.

32

Apples

Carrots

Broccoli & Cabbage

Vitamins and minerals

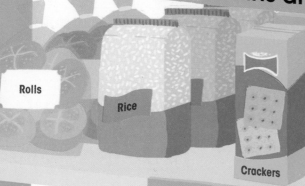

Rolls

Rice

Crackers

Chocolate Suckers

Carbohydrates

Nuts

Beans Beans ans

Proteins

Butter

Butter

Olive Oil

Olive Oil

Milk

Fats

Water

33

Dinner time!

To stay healthy, we can't just eat our favorite foods all the time. We need to eat a balanced amount of different food types.

This plate shows roughly how much of each type of food we should eat.

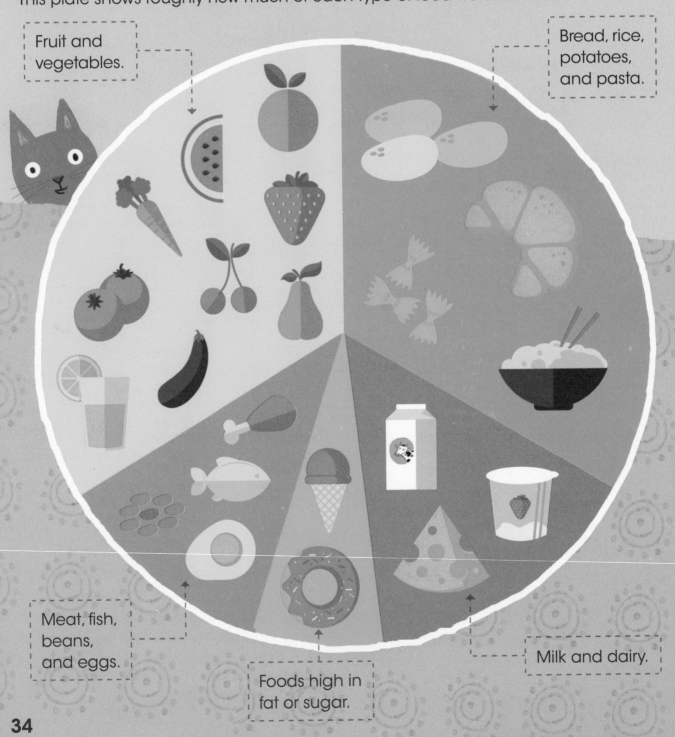

Fruit and vegetables.

Bread, rice, potatoes, and pasta.

Meat, fish, beans, and eggs.

Foods high in fat or sugar.

Milk and dairy.

Draw your favorite meal. What food types are there? Does it look like a healthy meal?

Your digestive system

When you eat your dinner, the food starts a long journey through your body's digestive system. It's a truly amazing food processor!

It's lunchtime!

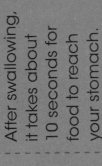

After swallowing, it takes about 10 seconds for food to reach your stomach.

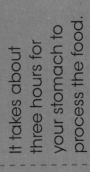

It takes about three hours for your stomach to process the food.

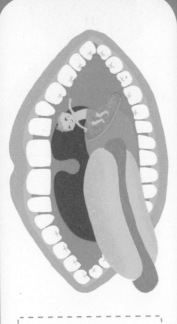

MOUTH
Most food is too big to be swallowed whole. Your teeth cut it into bite-size chunks and grind it into small pieces.

STOMACH
Your stomach squishes the food up with digestive juices to turn it into a liquid mush!

Liquid food spends about three hours passing through your small intestine.

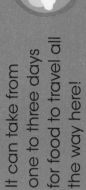

It can take from one to three days for food to travel all the way here!

SMALL INTESTINE
When it arrives here, the food has been broken down into tiny bits that can be used by your body.

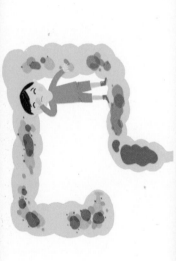

LARGE INTESTINE
Your large intestine turns the watery, leftover food waste into poo.

Quick digestion quiz
Food travels almost 30 feet through the tubes of the human digestive system.

TRUE

FALSE

Munching mouth

Hitch a ride with a mouthful of food to explore the body's digestive system. Your journey begins in the mouth!

Sharp front teeth are used to bite and slice up food.

I'm surfing a wave of yucky saliva!

Your back teeth are flat on the top. They grind food between them.

Salivary glands squirt out saliva, or spit, which mixes with the food and starts breaking it down or digesting it.

? Quick Quiz

How much saliva do you produce in one day?

A. Enough to fill a soda pop can. Eww!

B. Enough to fill a milk carton.

C. Enough to fill a swimming pool!

Your tongue is also used for tasting and talking.

Mixing chewed food with saliva makes it mushy and easy to swallow.

Your tongue is a big bundle of muscles that pushes food around for chewing or swallowing.

Squishy stomach

Once the food is chewed, your tongue pushes it to the back of your mouth, and it gets swallowed. Next stop—the stomach!

Your **throat** leads to your stomach, but you also use it to breathe in air.

Food is squeezed down a tube called the **esophagus** (say: uh-sof-a-gus) until it reaches the stomach.

Air travels down the **windpipe** to your lungs. Whenever you swallow, a flap closes off your windpipe so that food can't go the wrong way.

Quick, let's head for the stomach with the food.

Food this way!

Lung

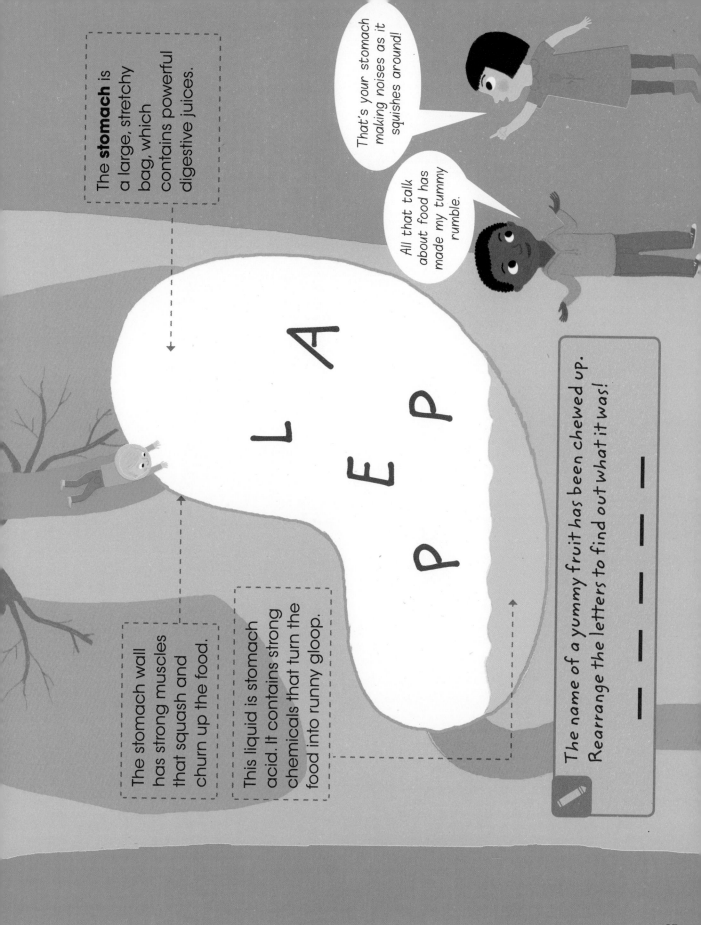

The **stomach** is a large, stretchy bag, which contains powerful digestive juices.

That's your stomach making noises as it squishes around!

All that talk about food has made my tummy rumble.

The stomach wall has strong muscles that squash and churn up the food.

This liquid is stomach acid. It contains strong chemicals that turn the food into runny gloop.

The name of a yummy fruit has been chewed up. Rearrange the letters to find out what it was!

L A E P P

_ _ _ _ _

When food goes wrong

HₒNNₙₙₖ!

Eating is usually fun, but sometimes eating food can have unexpected effects on your body!

Food can make you **fart**, creating smelly gas in your large intestine that then escapes with an embarrassing noise and a stink!

If you eat food that's gone bad or contains something harmful, your stomach knows. It takes action by making you **throw up**, sending the food back up the esophagus and out of your mouth. Yucky!

Sometimes, stomach acid goes the wrong way and comes back up from your stomach toward your throat. This causes **indigestion**—a horrible burning feeling in your chest.

A **burp** happens when gas or air from your stomach suddenly bubbles up out of your mouth. Sometimes this happens because you swallow air when you eat or drink too quickly.

BuuUrRpPpp!

Burping gets rid of one quart of gas from your stomach every day.

What embarrassing things have happened to you after eating or drinking? Keep a record here.

Today I drank a can of soda and burped in class five times! It was SO embarrassing!

Into the intestines!

After your food has been turned into gloop in the stomach, it sets off on a very long journey through the twisty tubes of your intestines, or guts.

Liquid food squeezes along inside the **small intestine**. The useful parts from the food are soaked up into your blood and travel to all the parts of your body, ready to be used.

I remember! Muscles squeeeeeze the food along.

Food can take up to six hours to pass through the small intestine into the large intestine.

This wormlike part between the small intestine and the large intestine is the appendix. No one is sure what it's for!

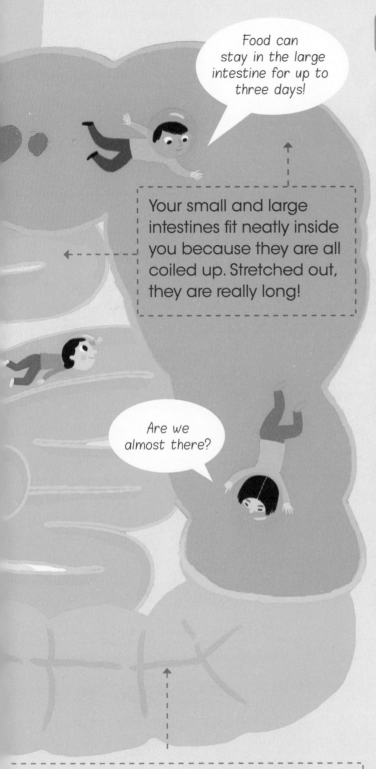

Food can stay in the large intestine for up to three days!

Your small and large intestines fit neatly inside you because they are all coiled up. Stretched out, they are really long!

Are we almost there?

Gigantic guts

Follow the steps to figure out how long your intestines are!

1. Measure your height:

   ....inches

2. Write your height x 4:

   ....inches

   (That's how long your small intestine is.)

3. Write your height x 1:

   ....inches
   (That's the length of your large intestine.)

4. Add the answers to 2 and 3 together to discover the total length of your intestines.

   ....inches

Wow, that is really LONG!

Once all the goodness has been taken out, the leftover food goes into the **large intestine**. Here, the pieces of food waste collect into lumps, ready to leave your body.

The Gassy Guts Hotel

Meet the guests who live in your guts! It's true—your large intestine is a bit like a hotel, where billions of bacteria come to stay.

Bacteria are tiny creatures that live inside everyone. They help you to digest your food and turn it into useful things, such as vitamins. They also help to keep dangerous germs away.

As the bacteria feed on the food gloop in your guts, they release waste gases that bubble along your intestines and then escape from your bottom as stinky farts.

Travel around the Gassy Guts Hotel, and answer TRUE or FALSE to the quiz questions.

1. Boys fart more than girls.
TRUE ⚪ FALSE ⚪

2. A fart's sound depends on the food it is made from.
TRUE ⚪ FALSE ⚪

3. You breathe in about a quart of other people's farts each day.
TRUE ⚪ FALSE ⚪

4. About a third of your poo is made of bacteria.

TRUE   FALSE

5. The older that you get, the more you fart.

TRUE   FALSE

Waste disposal

Remember that mouthful of food you were following? Now that all the goodness has been taken out, the leftover solid waste is ready to leave your large intestine—as poo!

LARGE INTESTINE

1. By the time food gets to your **large intestine**, your body has taken out all the useful parts. What's left are the parts you can't digest, known as fiber.

2. The intestine sucks water out of the waste food to dry it out.

3. It clumps into smelly lumps. As well as fiber, each lump contains gut bacteria.

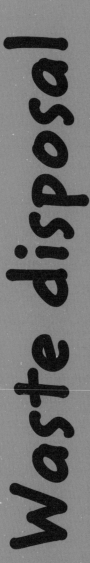

FROM THE SMALL INTESTINE

RECTUM

Fiber is good for you. It speeds up digestion to remove waste from your body. Check which two of these foods is high in fiber.

eggs ☐

vegetables ☐

wholewheat pasta ☐

EXIT
THIS
WAY

4. At the very end of the large intestine, the **rectum** stores the waste as poo until you go to the bathroom.

5. The bacteria in poo are what makes it stinky. Watch out! The bacteria in poo can make you sick if they get into your mouth. ALWAYS wash your hands after using the toilet!

Waterworks

So, what happens to the water you get from food and liquids? It travels from your small intestine into your blood and then to your kidneys.

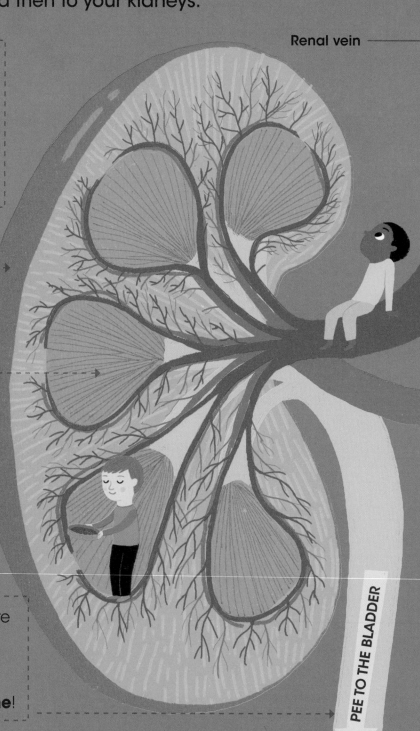

Renal vein

BLOOD TO THE BODY

Your body is mostly made of water. No matter how much water you take in, your **kidneys** make sure you have just the right amount.

They also control what chemicals are in your blood. The kidneys act like sieves to remove chemicals that shouldn't be there.

Extra water and waste chemicals travel out through the **ureter** (say: your-eat-er) to your **bladder** as **urine**!

PEE TO THE BLADDER

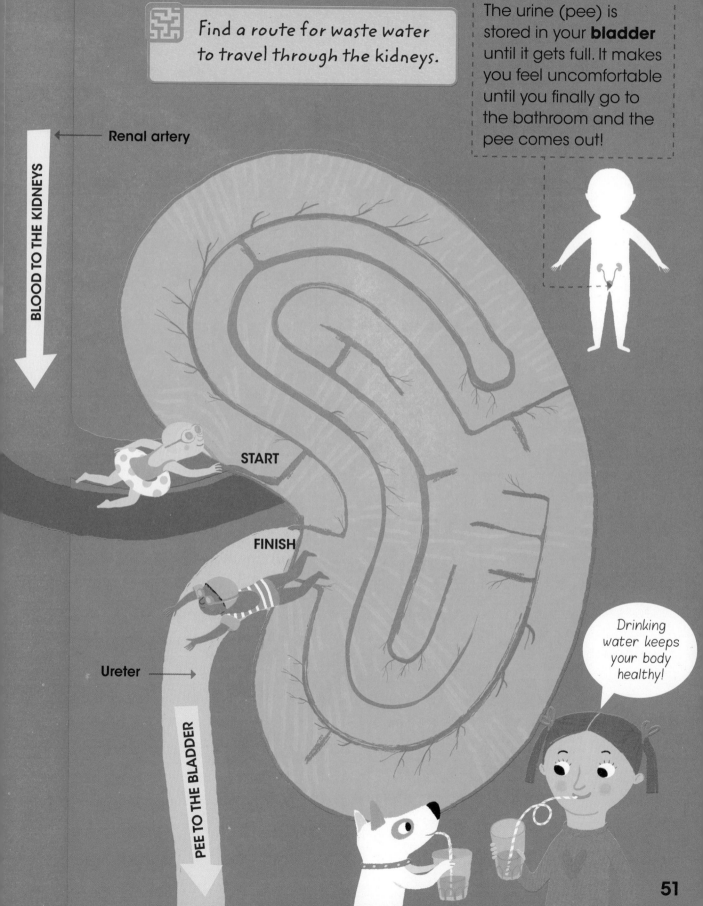

Your blood network

Each time your heart beats, it pumps blood all around your body. The blood flows through a network of tubes called blood vessels.

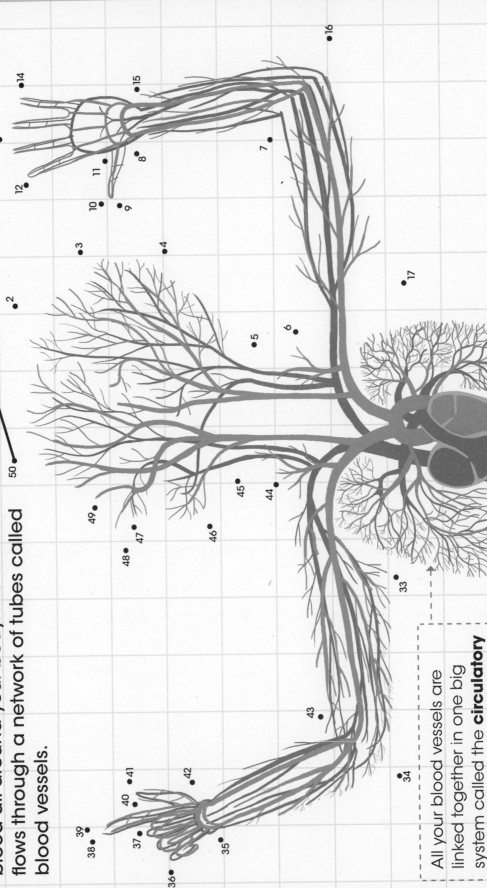

All your blood vessels are linked together in one big system called the **circulatory system**. It carries blood close to every cell in your body, from head to toe.

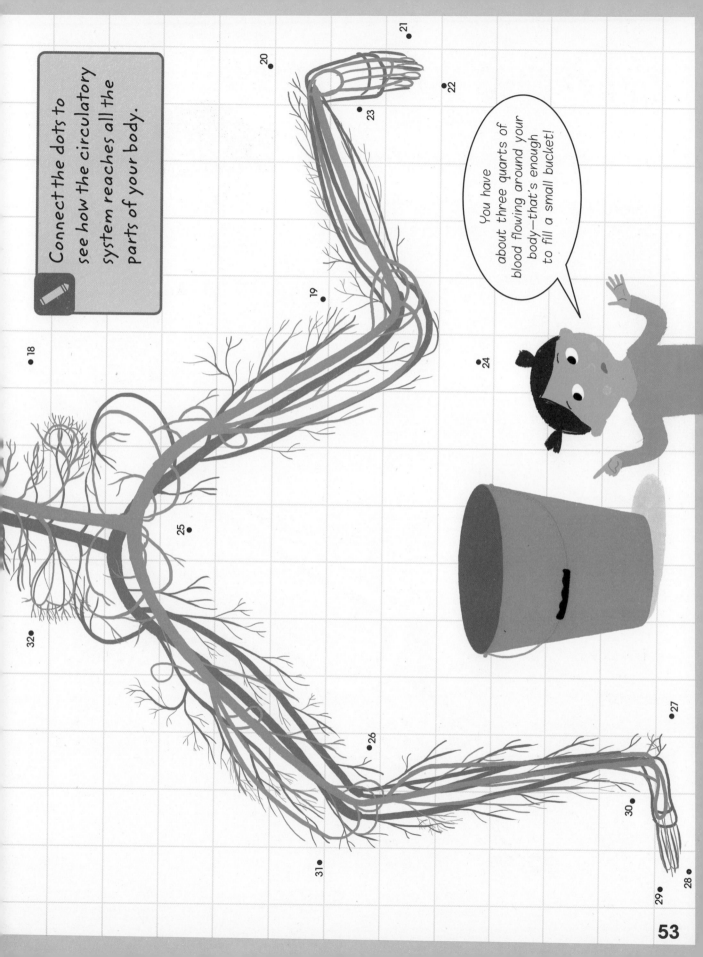

Connect the dots to see how the circulatory system reaches all the parts of your body.

You have about three quarts of blood flowing around your body—that's enough to fill a small bucket!

53

Blood vessels

Your heart pumps blood nonstop around your circulatory system. This network is so huge that if the **blood vessels** were laid out end to end, they would stretch around the Earth an incredible two-and-a-half times!

Blood vessels leading out of the heart are called **arteries**.

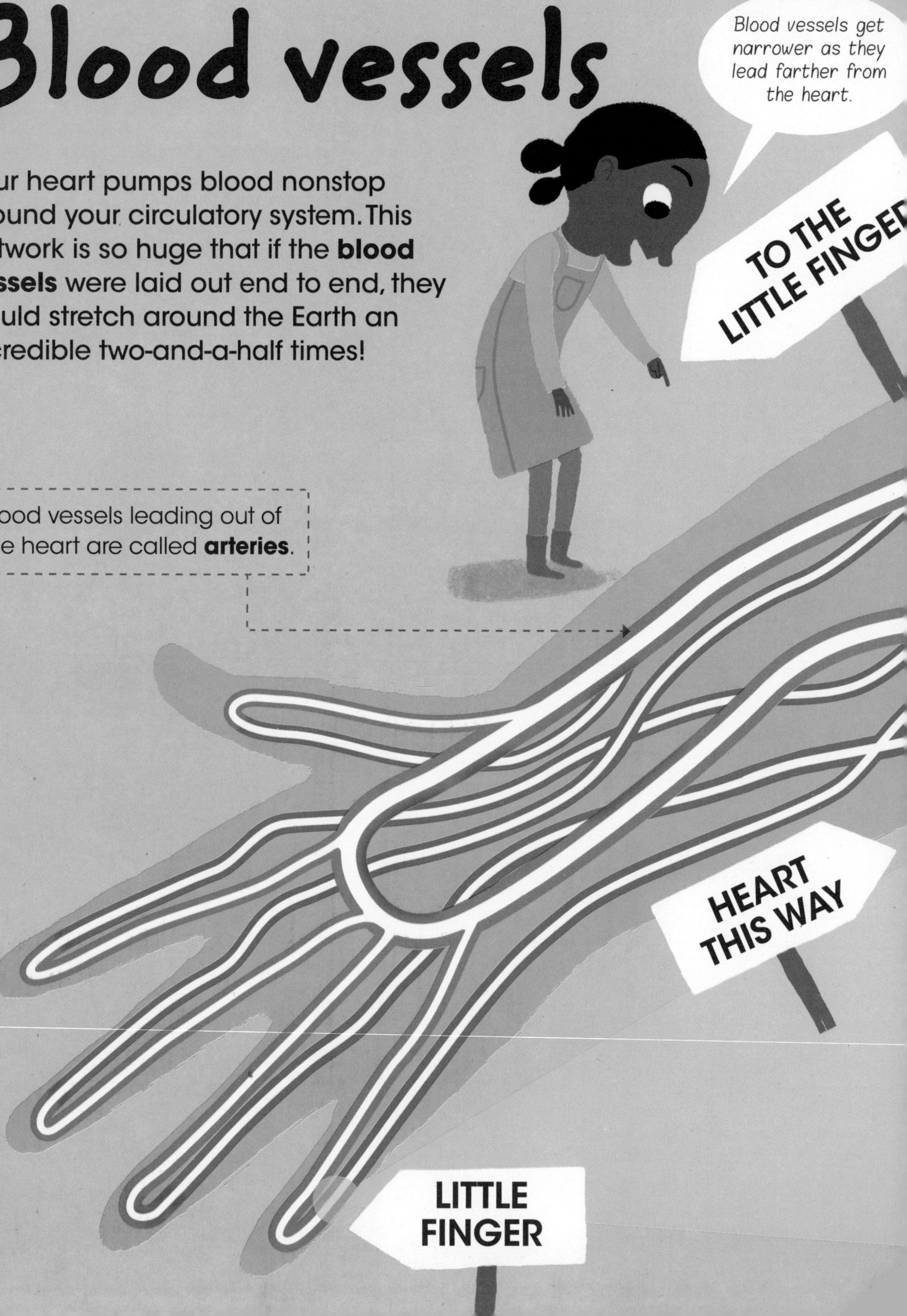

Blood vessels get narrower as they lead farther from the heart.

TO THE LITTLE FINGER

HEART THIS WAY

LITTLE FINGER

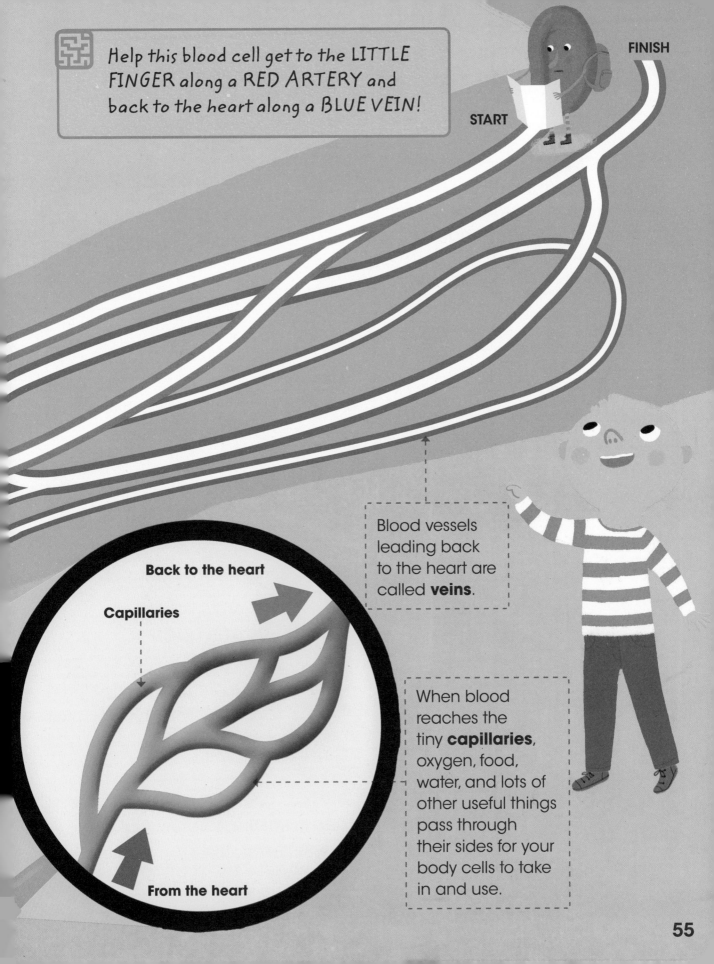

Help this blood cell get to the LITTLE FINGER along a RED ARTERY and back to the heart along a BLUE VEIN!

START

FINISH

Blood vessels leading back to the heart are called **veins**.

Back to the heart

Capillaries

From the heart

When blood reaches the tiny **capillaries**, oxygen, food, water, and lots of other useful things pass through their sides for your body cells to take in and use.

Blood delivers

Around the clock, your blood delivers all the stuff your body needs. It does lots of other useful jobs, too. Discover what your blood delivery service carries around the body.

Oxygen is a gas in the air that we breathe in. Every cell needs oxygen to work.

Cells need **food** to make them work.

Cells need **water**. It is used to make things like tears, sweat, saliva—and blood, too!

Germ-fighting cells in your blood protect you from germs.

Your blood carries a **first-aid kit** to help repair wounds and make scabs.

Inside a drop of blood

Blood looks red and runny, but what's it actually made of? Let's zoom in and get to know the millions of microscopic cells that float about in a single drop of blood.

There's so much packed into just one tiny drop of blood!

Wow! Look at all those red blood cells.

Red blood cells

Cells in one drop: roughly 300 million.
Description: round, flat and, um ... red!
Job: carrying oxygen and delivering it to all the cells in the body.

Platelets

Cells in one drop: up to 15 million.
Description: small, round, and flat like a plate—they stretch out long fingers when they need to mend a wound.
Job: clumping together to build scabs and heal cuts.

From the heart

Your heart has two sides that work together.
They pump blood to your lungs to pick up oxygen.
Then they send the blood around the body.

Take a ride on a **red blood cell.**

1. The right-hand side pumps red blood cells to your **lungs**.

Let's hitch a ride on a red blood cell to see where it goes.

First stop, the heart!

RIGHT SIDE

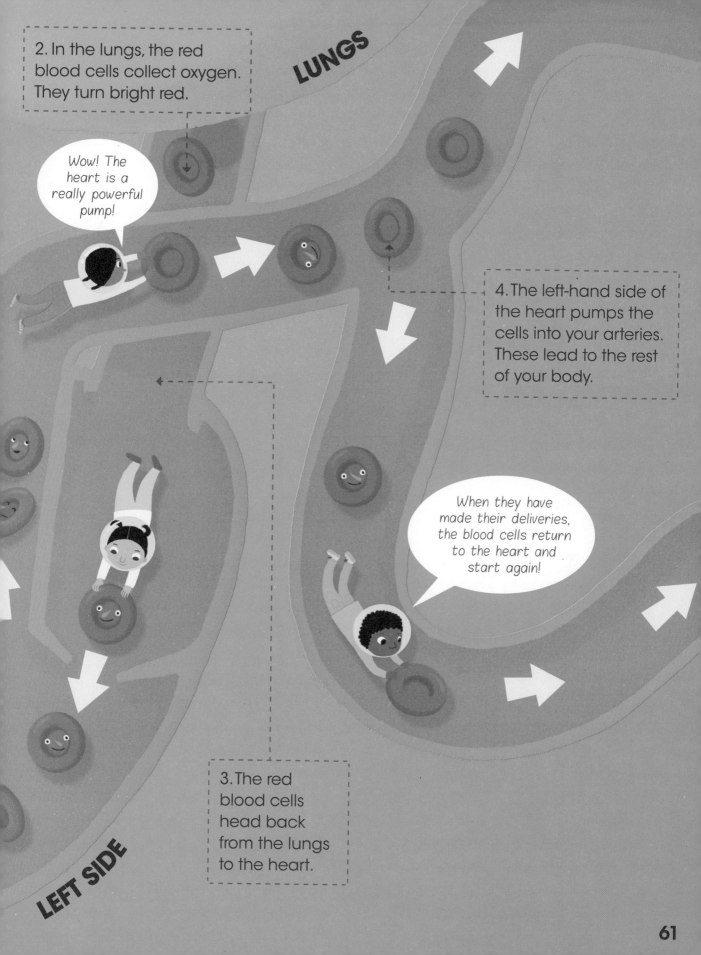

Your pulse

Every time your heart squeezes to pump blood around your body, it produces a heartbeat. Your pulse rate is the number of times your heart beats in one minute.

Your cells need more oxygen and food when you exercise. So your heart beats faster to pump more blood around your body.

What happens to your pulse rate when you exercise? Do this fun experiment to find out!

1. First, find out your normal pulse rate. Stick out one hand, palm up, and press two fingers of your other hand onto the wrist, like this.

2. Can you feel a regular bump? That's your pulse. Use a watch and count how many times your pulse bumps in one minute:

_ _ _ beats per minute.

3. Now, take your pulse rate before and after each of these exercises. Rest for five minutes between each exercise to write in your results.

One minute of running

BEFORE: ....

AFTER: ....

One minute of jumping rope
BEFORE: ....
AFTER: ....

One minute of dancing
BEFORE: ....
AFTER: ....

One minute of jumping jacks
BEFORE: ....
AFTER: ....

Hard-working heart

Your heart is an incredibly hard-working muscle.
Even when you are sitting very still, it's hard at
work, beating around 70 times every minute.

Color the 70 little heartbeats in red.
How many can you do in one minute?

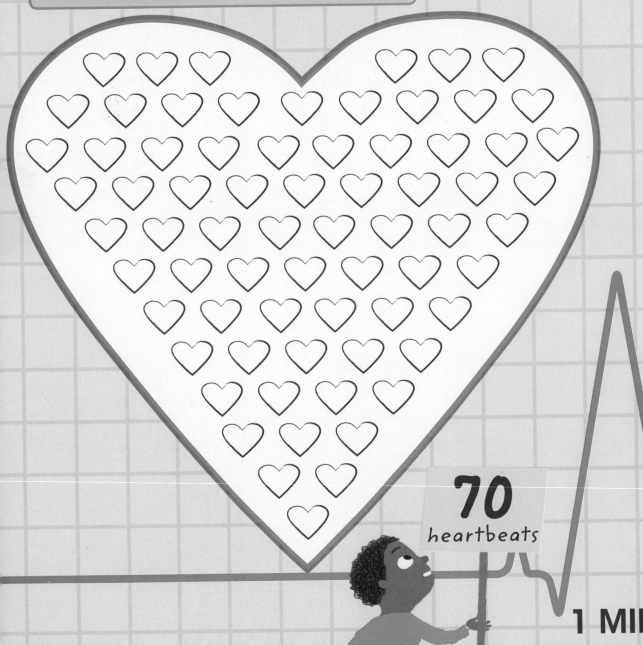

70 heartbeats

1 MINUT

Doctors can listen to our hearts with a **stethoscope** to make sure that they are working properly. It makes the sounds louder and easier to hear.

Your heart is beating before you are even born. The heart might beat up to three billion times (3,000,000,000) in an average lifetime.

4,200
heartbeats

100,800
heartbeats

1 HOUR

1 DAY

Breathing

Take a deep breath. Your **lungs** have just filled up with air, and oxygen has been added to your blood. Now breathe the rest of the air back out!

AIR

1. **Air** gets into your body through your **nose** and **mouth**.

LUNG

2. The air travels down your throat and then continues on through the **trachea** (say: tra-kee-a), or windpipe.

3. The trachea splits into two tubes, each leading into one of your two **lungs**. The tubes are called **bronchi** (say: brong-key).

Cool! Your body gets its oxygen from air.

4. The **bronchi** branch off into thousands of smaller tubes—the **bronchioles** (say: brong-key-oles).

DIAPHRAGM

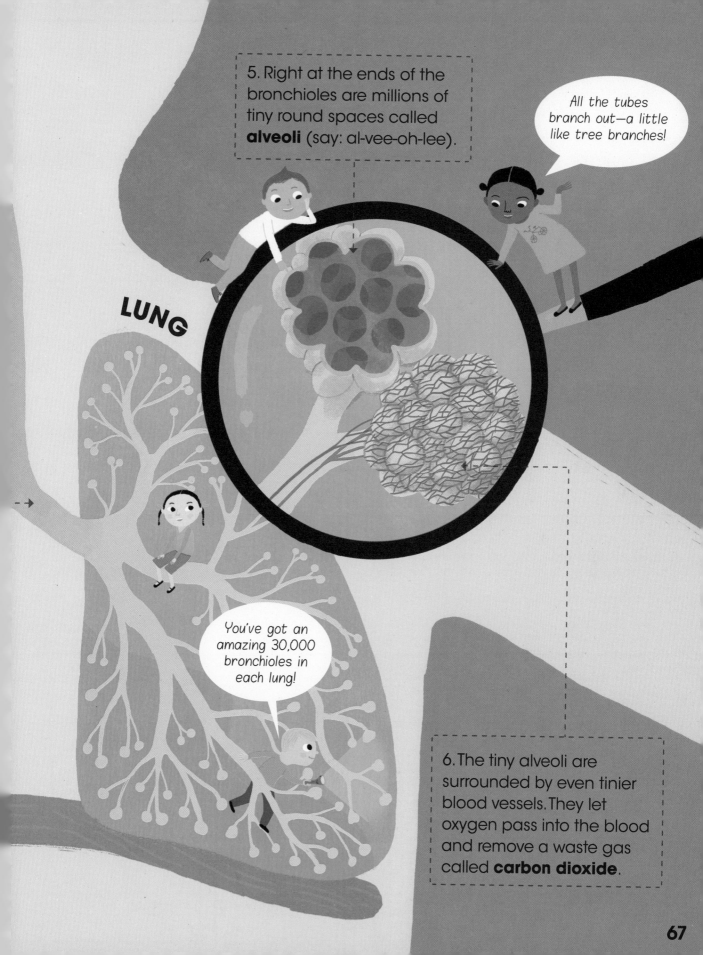

Hiccups!

However hard you try, you can't stop a hiccup. It's a sudden, jerky breath that shakes your body from the inside. But why do we get hiccups?

1. Hiccups happen in a big, stretchy breathing muscle called the **diaphragm** (say "die-a-fram"). It's a dome-shaped muscle, just under your lungs.

2. To make you breathe in, the diaphragm muscle pulls down. This makes your lungs open to suck air in.

 Color in this comic strip of ways to stop hiccups. Which have you tried? Did it work?

BREATHING IN

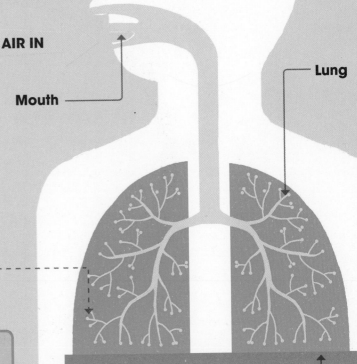

AIR IN

Mouth

Lung

Diaphragm

Hic!

Drink a glass of water.

Hold your breath.

BREATHING OUT

Hic!

AIR OUT

Windpipe

3. To make you breathe out, the diaphragm relaxes and moves back up. Your lungs get smaller and push air out.

4. If you eat or drink too fast, the diaphragm can jerk up and down. This makes you breathe in suddenly. To keep you from choking in case you accidently breathe in food, your body quickly closes your windpipe. That's what makes the "hic" sound.

Sing!   A sudden surprise!

Brain and senses

Inside your head is the brain, which is the control center for your body. The brain takes in information from your body and its senses, including your eyes, ears, nose, tongue, and skin.

Your **brain** works like a computer. It receives information from your senses and uses it to decide what to do.

**Thinking ...
... deciding ...
doing ...
it's an apple!**

Instructions to Body
1. Find money—it's in your pocket.
2. Buy apple.
3. Eat apple—yummy!

The brain sends out signals to make your body move, walk, or talk. It really is the boss!

Another great idea of mine!

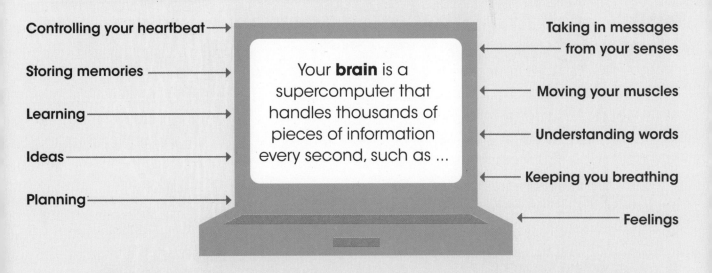

Controlling your heartbeat →

Storing memories →

Learning →

Ideas →

Planning →

Your **brain** is a supercomputer that handles thousands of pieces of information every second, such as ...

← Taking in messages from your senses

← Moving your muscles

← Understanding words

← Keeping you breathing

← Feelings

How good is your brain at remembering? Look at these 10 objects for 10 seconds. Cover them and write down as many as you can remember!

1 ....
2 ....
3 ....
4 ....
5 ....

6 ....
7 ....
8 ....
9 ....
10 ....

How did you score?

10/10 Superbrain!

5 to 8 Totally brainy

1 to 4 Brain strain!

Take a brain tour

Your brain is made up of many parts, and the brain cells in different areas of the brain have special jobs. Explore the brain with this map.

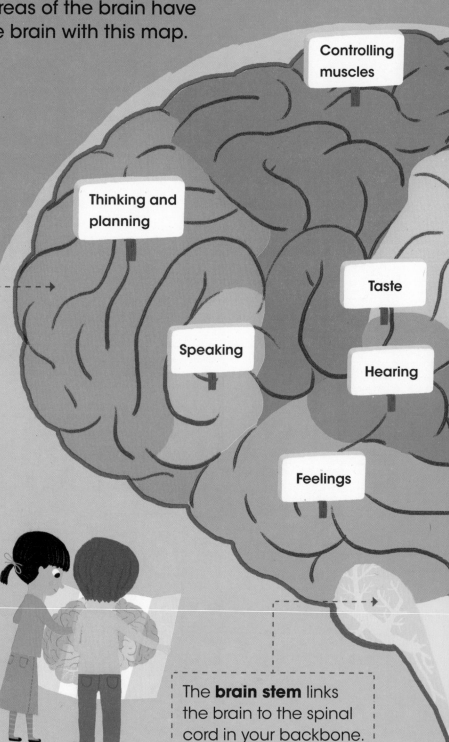

The **cerebrum** (say: se-ree-brum) makes up most of your brain. It controls your body when you choose to do things.

The bumpy, wrinkly outer layer of the cerebrum is called the **cerebral cortex** (say: se-ree-bral core-tex). It's used for sensing, thinking, and learning.

Controlling muscles

Thinking and planning

Taste

Speaking

Hearing

Feelings

The **brain stem** links the brain to the spinal cord in your backbone.

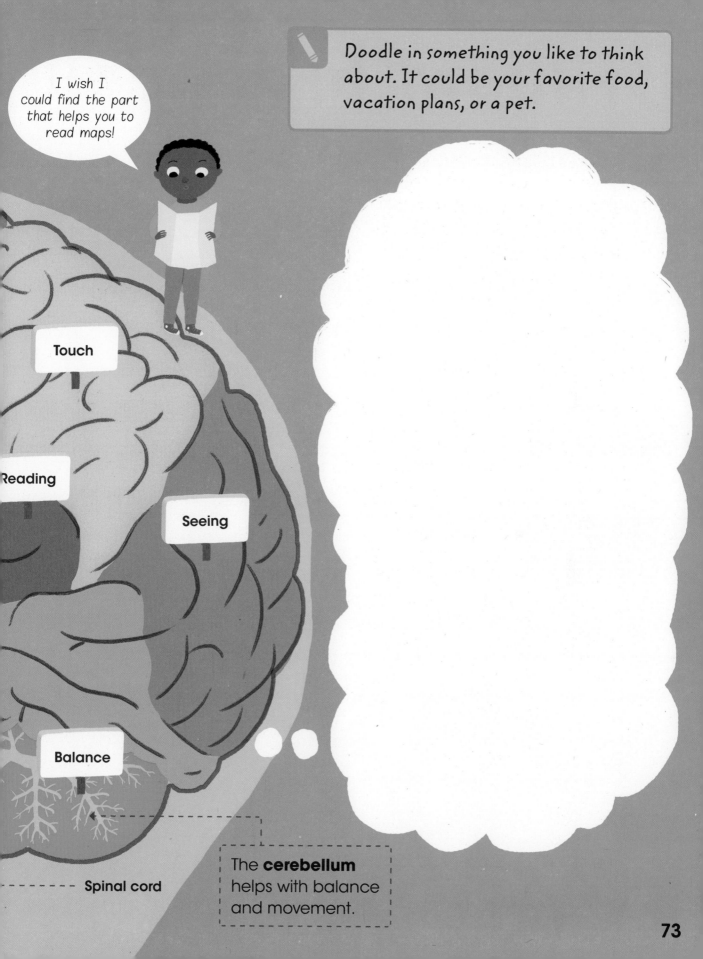

Brilliant brain cells

Your brain has billions of brain cells called neurons. Each neuron is like a tiny octopus, with lots of tentacles that reach out to link it with other brain cells.

Your brain must be very clever to send messages through this tangled maze!

 The alarm clock is ringing! Find a way through this tangle of neurons to choose what you'd like to do.

There may be one hundred billion **neurons** in the human brain.

START

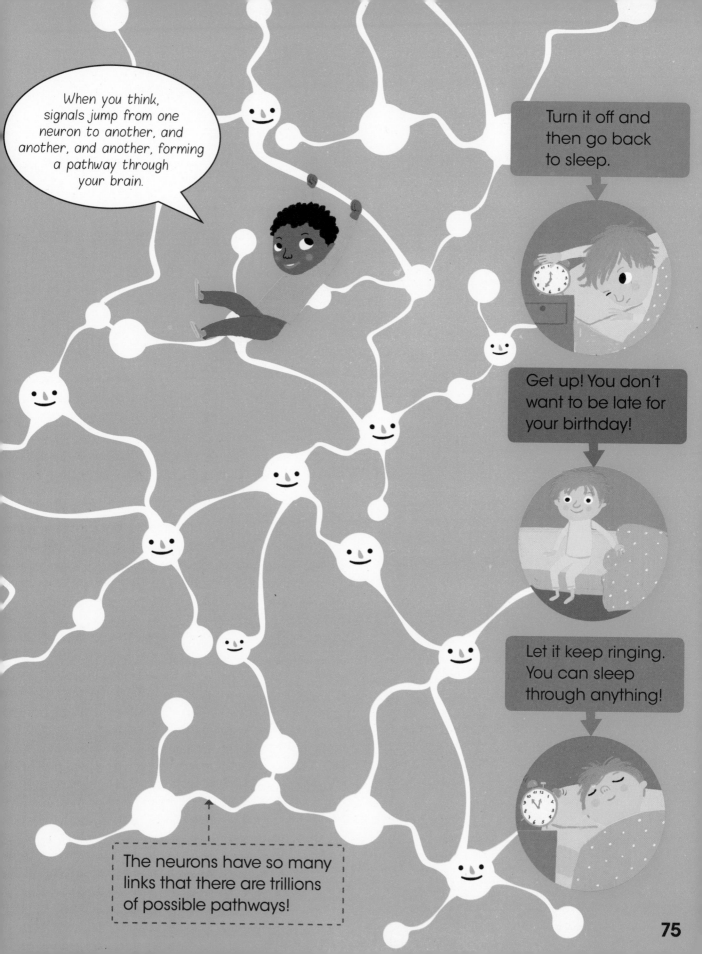

Your nerve network

A network of cells called nerves carries information and messages between your body and your brain. It's called the nervous system—and it's superfast!

Nerves pick up information from your eyes, ears, tongue, nose, and touch sensors all over your skin.

Your **nervous system** carries this information to your brain.

Your **nervous system** carries messages between your **brain** and your body.

You have just caught the ball!

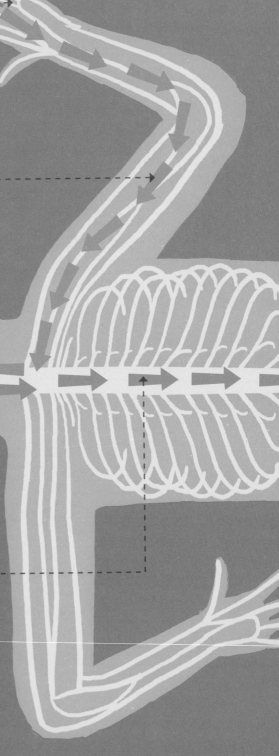

Make those feet move!

The **spinal cord** is a big bundle of nerves that runs down your back, inside your backbone. Lots of smaller nerve pathways branch off from it.

Your nervous system stretches from head to toe.

Nerve signals can travel very fast—it can take just a fraction of a second for your brain to sense something, decide what to do, and act on it.

Your nervous system is made of neurons—the same as the cells in the brain.

Write a message from the brain to a part of the body. What will you tell it to do?

Message from: The Brain

To: _____ (body part)

Zzzzzzzzzz ...

When you sleep, you don't seem to hear, see, or notice things around you. But inside your skull, your brain is still working—all around the clock!

Your **brain** keeps working to control things like body heat, heartbeat, and breathing. It also keeps alert to danger.

A really loud noise could signal danger, so your brain wakes you up.

Scientists think that while you sleep, your brain sorts through the things it has stored, keeping important stuff in your memory and throwing the rest away.

Your brain likes to keep things very organized!

You **dream** while you sleep. Dreams can be very weird! Scientists think that these strange stories happen as your brain sorts through your memories and feelings.

Dreams are often scrambled and mixed up.

Magical or totally impossible things can happen in your dreams!

Dreams sometimes include people, places, and events from real life.

Create a dream diary. Write down your dreams as soon as you wake up—before you forget them!

My weirdest dream: _

_ _

My funniest dream: _

_ _

My scariest dream: _

_ _

Inside your eye

From the moment you open your eyes in the morning to when you close them at night, they take pictures of the world around you and send them to your brain.

1. Light rays pass through the pupil and the lens.

Our eyes need light to see. Light rays come from the sun, light bulbs or even a flashlight. Rays of light bounce off of things and into your eyes.

The **lens** works like a camera lens to bring images into focus.

The **pupil** is the dark circle in the middle of the eye. It can be made smaller or bigger to let more or less light in.

Now I see how it works.

The **iris** controls how much light comes into the eye by changing the size of the pupil.

Hey—it's all upside down!

What is this eye looking at? Connect the dots and then turn the page around to find out!

2. As light rays enter the eyeball, they cross over before they land on your retina to create an upside-down picture.

The **retina** at the back of your eye is made of light-sensitive cells.

3. Nerve cells in the retina turn the patterns of light into signals.

4. The signals zoom along the **optic nerve** to the brain. It flips the picture the right way around and figures out what it is.

Your **eyeball** is filled with a clear jelly that lets light through.

TO THE BRAIN

Goofy gallery

Your brain is brilliant at sorting out all the signals from your eyes. But sometimes even your clever brain can't figure out what it's seeing!

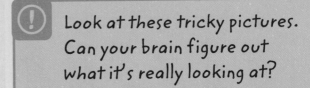

Look at these tricky pictures. Can your brain figure out what it's really looking at?

Look at these squares. Can you see gray dots appear?

Which of the two blue trees is bigger? Measure them to find out.

Your brain knows that things should look smaller if they are far away, so it thinks the faraway tree must be the biggest.

Do the rows of tiles go across at different angles?

Do you see a duck or a rabbit? Or does it flip between the two?

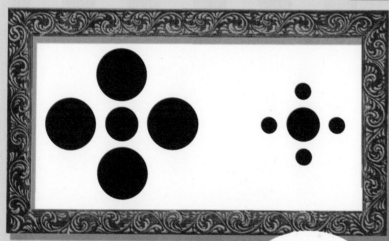

Look at the two dots in the middle of these patterns. Which one is bigger? Now measure them with a ruler.

I need a ruler to check this out!

Listen!

Your ears are truly amazing, picking up all the sounds around you, from soft sounds like the wind in the trees, to loud noises like a drum.

The smallest bone in your body is found inside your ear.

The **ear canal** is a tunnel leading inside your ear.

Let's make some noise!

Sound travels as a series of ripples, or sound waves, in the air.

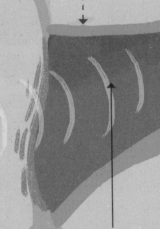

Outer ear

Your ears are dish-shaped to catch sound waves in the air.

Your **eardrum** is a thin, tightly stretched skin—like the skin of a drum!

When the sound waves hit your eardrum, they make it vibrate (shake to and fro).

Tiny hairs inside the **cochlea** sense the vibrations and turn them into nerve signals.

It sounds like it's dinner time!

Inner ear

The nerve signals go to your brain, which makes sense of the sound signals.

Middle ear

Tiny ear bones called **ossicles** (say: oss-ick-culs) carry the vibrations to the spiral-shaped cochlea.

La la la!

 Gently put your hand on your throat and sing or talk. Can you feel the sound vibrations?

Know your nose

Smells really do get up your nose! You smell things when tiny bits of them float into your nostrils. That's everything from fresh bread to stinky socks!

Nearly three inches inside your nostrils there is a patch of smell-detecting cells.

When something smelly touches the smell-detecting cells, they send signals along nerves to the brain.

Mmmmm! That smells like bread. Can I have a slice, please?

Some very small pieces of bread make their way to your nose, especially when you breathe in.

The very tiny pieces of bread are far too small to see.

The smell of this freshly baked bread is actually made of tiny molecules of bread that float into the air.

Nasty smells are useful, too. They tell us when something is rotten, burning—or needs a wash!

Sense of smell experiment

Collect some smelly things from the list here, and put them in separate plastic cups.

1. Ask friends or family members to take turns putting on a blindfold and then sniffing each smelly thing.

2. Can they tell you what each one is just by sense of smell? Write down their answers.

How many did they get right? Who has the best sense of smell?

You will need

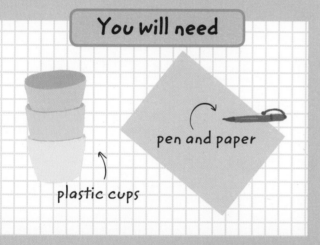

pen and paper

plastic cups

Smelly things

vinegar

coffee

lemon

chocolate bar

pencil and pencil shavings

rose petals

onion

banana

peppermints

orange

Mmmm, I'm smelling my favorite smell. CHOCOLATE!

Tasty!

You have about 10,000 tiny taste buds on your tongue. The nerves in your taste buds send signals to your brain about what's in your mouth.

Taste buds

Your tongue has tiny bumps all over it. The **taste buds** are in these bumps. When you eat, saliva (spit) washes food into the bumps, and it touches the taste buds.

More than three-quarters of what you taste actually comes from your sense of smell. As you eat, you smell your food, too. That's why your food isn't as tasty when you have a cold—your smell cells are blocked with snot!

Yum! Salty, like potato chips!

Umami – that's savory, like strong cheese!

Sour like lemons!

I can't taste a thing!

Your taste buds can sense five main tastes: sweet, sour, salt, bitter, and umami (say: ooo-ma-me).

Keep in touch

Just imagine touching something really hot, if you didn't know it was hot! Sensors in our skin keep us aware of danger—they also help us to feel the world around us.

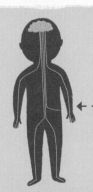

The skin all over your body is full of touch sensors, made of special cells that send information to your brain.

? Match the children in the park to what their sense of touch is telling them.

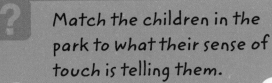

Pain .... *Ouch! That's spiky.*

Cold .... *Ahh, lovely and cool.*

Heat .... *Phew! I'm hot.*

Pressure ... *I'm being pulled along!*

Your skin has touch sensors to feel cold, heat, pain, and pressure.

Your senses really keep you in touch with the world.

Quick reactions

How quickly you can react depends on how fast your brain can tell your body what to do. Your body also has superfast automatic reactions, called **reflexes**.

Reaction time test

Test how quick your reactions are with this fun experiment!

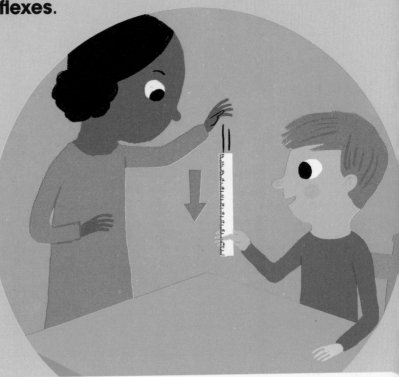

1. Ask a friend to hold a ruler, with the low numbers at the bottom end.

2. Hold your hand open around the bottom of the ruler.

3. Ask your friend to drop the ruler. As soon as you see it fall, grab it!

4. The number you grab gives you a score. Lower numbers mean faster reactions.

Try it three times, and write down your results. Then try testing different people to see who is the fastest.

Reaction results

Number:

Name: 1   2   3

Me _____ ◯ ◯ ◯

_____ ◯ ◯ ◯

_____ ◯ ◯ ◯

_____ ◯ ◯ ◯

_____ ◯ ◯ ◯

_____ ◯ ◯ ◯

Who has the fastest reactions?

_____

Reflexes are reactions that you don't control. They can automatically protect you when there's not enough time for messages to get to your brain and back.

Your blink reflex makes you automatically close your eyelids when something comes near them.

Reflexes help to protect us in emergencies.

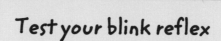

Test your blink reflex

Stand behind a window, and ask a friend to go on the other side and throw cotton balls toward your face.

Can you resist your blink reflex and keep your eyes open the whole time?

Under your skin

Yuck! I've just stepped in some sweat!

Your skin provides a tough, flexible covering for your body. It does lots of useful jobs, too. In fact, there's a lot more to your skin than what you can see on the surface!

The thinner top layer of your skin is called the **epidermis** (say: ep-i-der-miss).

The surface of your skin is a layer of dead, flattened cells. These flake off and get replaced by more from below.

The thicker layer underneath is called the **dermis** (say: der-miss).

There's a lot to see under your skin!

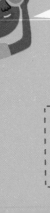

Sweat glands make and release sweat to holes on the surface called **pores**.

Blood vessels bring food and oxygen to your skin cells and carry away waste.

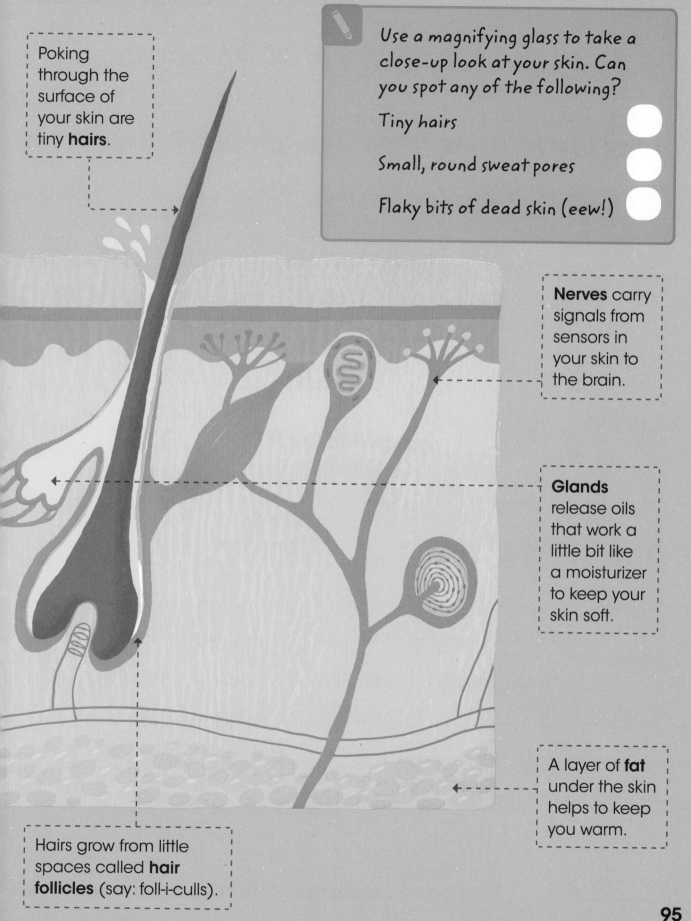

Poking through the surface of your skin are tiny **hairs**.

Use a magnifying glass to take a close-up look at your skin. Can you spot any of the following?

Tiny hairs

Small, round sweat pores

Flaky bits of dead skin (eew!)

Nerves carry signals from sensors in your skin to the brain.

Glands release oils that work a little bit like a moisturizer to keep your skin soft.

A layer of **fat** under the skin helps to keep you warm.

Hairs grow from little spaces called **hair follicles** (say: foll-i-culls).

Your super skin

Groups of cells make up organs with special jobs to do, such as your heart. Did you know that your skin is your body's largest organ, with lots of important jobs to do?

Your skin is like a superhero. Color in this comic strip to discover some of the great jobs your super skin does!

It keeps your body parts safe inside and stops them from drying out.

It keeps dirt and germs out of your body.

It helps you to sense the world around you.

It may be dark, but my sense of touch will easily find you!

Wow! Super senses!

It's superflexible so you can pull all those fancy superhero moves.

Gasp! It's super skin to the rescue!

It can keep you warm and help you to cool down.

Another happy ending— thanks to my superpowers!

Get a grip!

The skin on the palms of your hands and the soles of your feet has little ridges to give you better grip. The best way to see this is to take a close look at your fingertips.

Everyone has their own special pattern of lines and ridges on their fingertips.

The ridges have lots of sweat pores. They release sweat to keep the skin very slightly damp. This helps us to grip the surface of some objects.

Most of your body is covered with small hairs, but not your fingertips, the palms of your hands, or the soles of your feet.

Compare your fingerprints with family or friends. See—they are all different!

Use a washable pen to color the top part of your thumb. Then press it down on the space below. Do the same for the rest of your fingers.

THUMB	FINGER 1	FINGER 2	FINGER 3	FINGER 4

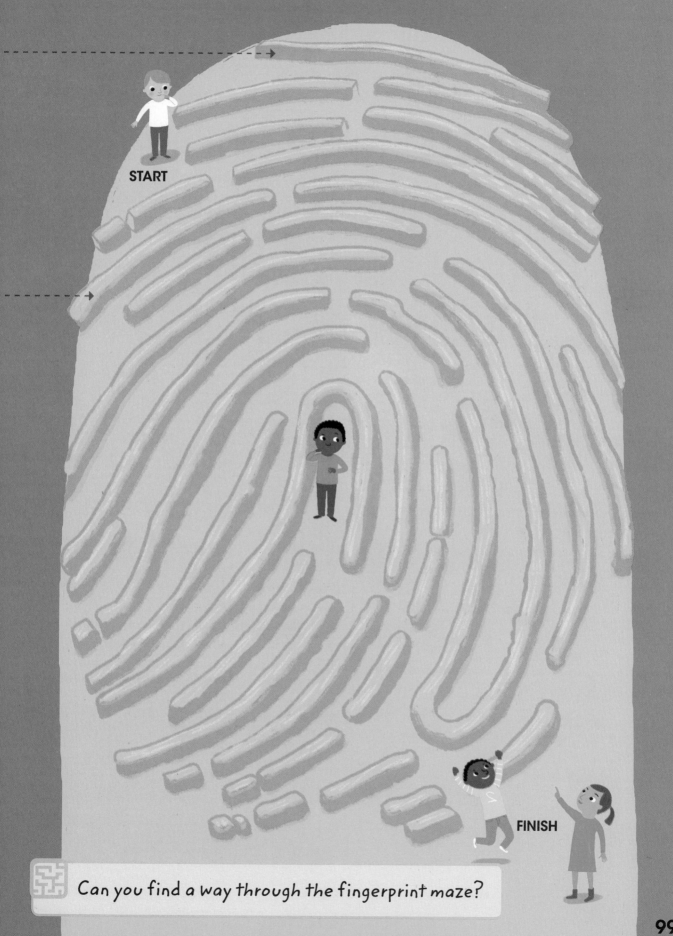

START

FINISH

Can you find a way through the fingerprint maze?

First-aid kit

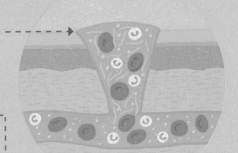

A scab works a bit like a bandage!

If you cut yourself, blood flows out from under your skin. Luckily, your skin has its own first-aid kit. It makes a scab to stop the leak and starts healing the cut.

First-aid Kit
Ingredients for making scabs:

● **Red blood cells**

● **Disk-shaped platelets**

● **Stringy, sticky fibrin threads**

1. Emergency! A net of sticky fibrin threads and small, plate-shaped cells called platelets plug the leak.

It can take from five days to six weeks for a cut to heal.

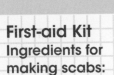

A cut breaks blood vessels under the skin, and red blood cells pour out.

2. Stop the leak. The cut is properly sealed off as the mesh of ingredients starts to dry out, forming a thick clot.

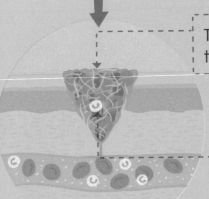

The net holds back the red blood cells.

White blood cells fight any germs in the area.

3. Making a scab. Protected by the scab, the skin beneath repairs itself. When it's done the scab falls off.

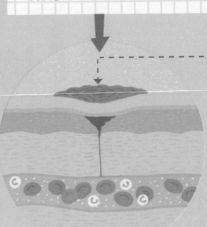

The surface of the clot dries and hardens to form a scab.

Make your own gross scab by following the steps below. Then show it to your friends!

Don't worry banana, you'll make a full recovery!

You will need:

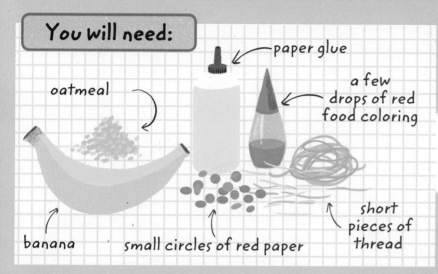

paper glue

a few drops of red food coloring

oatmeal

banana

small circles of red paper

short pieces of thread

1

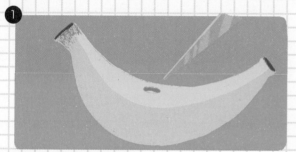

Ask an adult to help you make a hole in a banana (leave the skin on). This is the "cut" you will fix!

2

Mix some paper glue with the thread and red food coloring to make the fibrin.

3

Add oatmeal for platelets and the small red paper circles as red blood cells.

4

Mix all the scab ingredients together. Then use the mixture to fill and cover the hole.

5

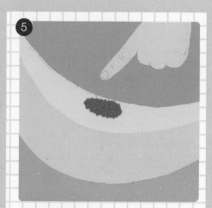

Let it dry and watch it form into a crispy scab. Gross!

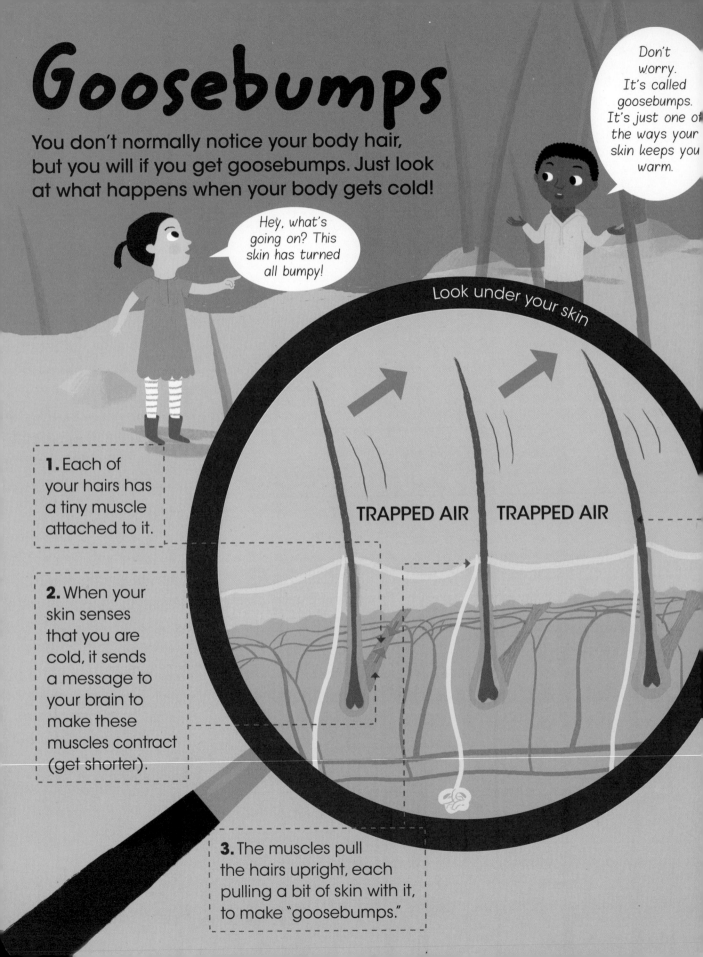

All the little hairs are standing up!

You get goosebumps when you feel scared, too. Your hairs stand up to make you seem bigger.

Animals get goose bumps, too. Look at this scaredy cat!

4. The hairs stand on end and trap air next to your body to keep you warm, like a woolly sweater.

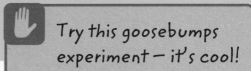

1

Pour some tap water into a bowl and add ice cubes. Wait until the ice has made the water really cold.

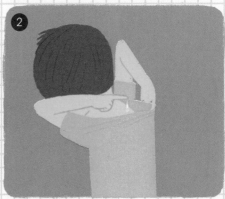

2

Dip a finger in, and use it to dribble a few drops of the icy water down your back. Brrrr!

3

Watch the hair and skin on your arms. Did you get goosebumps?

Hot and cold

To keep healthy, your body needs to stay at about the same temperature. If you get too hot, your skin has some cool tricks to turn down the temperature!

When it's hot, the hairs on your skin lay flat. It's like taking a sweater off on a sunny day!

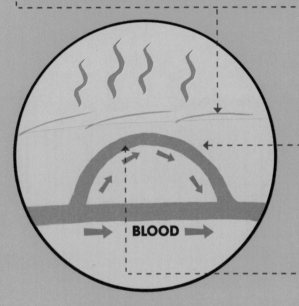

BLOOD

Blood vessels near the surface of your skin become wider, letting more blood flow through.

Blood near the surface loses heat, cooling you down.

Your skin is covered with millions of tiny holes called **sweat pores**. These lead to **sweat glands** under the surface of your skin.

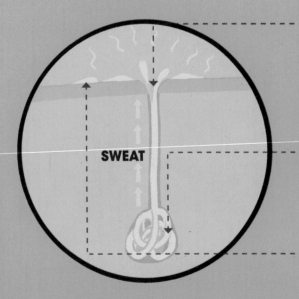

SWEAT

Your **sweat glands** regularly release liquid sweat onto the surface of your skin. When you get hot, they can produce up to a quart of sweat in an hour.

As the **sweat** dries off, it cools down your skin and your body.

When it's cold, your body keeps blood away from the surface of your skin, where it would lose some heat.

BLOOD

Blood vessels become narrower, so less blood can flow through. This can make you look paler.

Quick quiz

Chill out or work up a sweat by checking the correct answers below!

1. You sweat all the time, not just on hot days.

TRUE FALSE

2. Sweating releases hot water onto your skin to keep you warm.

TRUE FALSE

3. Your skin is covered with more than two million sweat pores.

TRUE FALSE

Hair safari

Most of us have hair on our head, but we've also got tiny hairs all over our body. The thickest and longest hairs are found on the head. Take a closer look!

Most of your hair is not living cells. It's made of a tough material called keratin (say: care-a-tin).

Eek! This hair is flexible and wobbly!

It's like a jungle down here.

A typical person has about 100,000 head hairs.

The hairs on your head are very close together, with up to 2,200 hairs in every square inch.

Take a close look at a friend's head hair with a magnifying glass. What can you see close up?

Your hair grows about half an inch every month!

Each hair root is alive, but the rest of your hair cells are dead.

Hairs grow from hair follicles. You've got about five million follicles under your skin!

Your hair cells grow from this **hair root**.

Hair types salon

Draw in the different hair types for the people below.

Some people have straight hair, while others have wavy or curly hair. The type of hair you have depends on the shape of the hairs and how they grow out of your skin.

Draw in some straight hair.

Let's get styling!

STRAIGHT HAIR

Straight hairs have a round shape. They grow from hair follicles with a round shape.

WAVY HAIR

Wavy hairs are a little flatter than straight hair. They grow from hair follicles that are slightly more squished.

Draw in some curly hair.

CURLY HAIR

Curly hairs are very flat and grow out of long, thin hair follicles.

Nifty nails

Tigers have claws, horses have hooves, but humans have fingernails and toenails. These hard coverings help to protect the tips of your fingers and toes.

New nail cells grow out from an area called the **nail root**.

This end of the nail is called the **free edge**. It's the part that sticks out more as the nail grows.

Just like your hair, your nails are made out of superstrong **keratin**.

Cuticle

Toenails grow more slowly than fingernails.

The hard surface of the nail is made of dead cells and is called the **nail plate**.

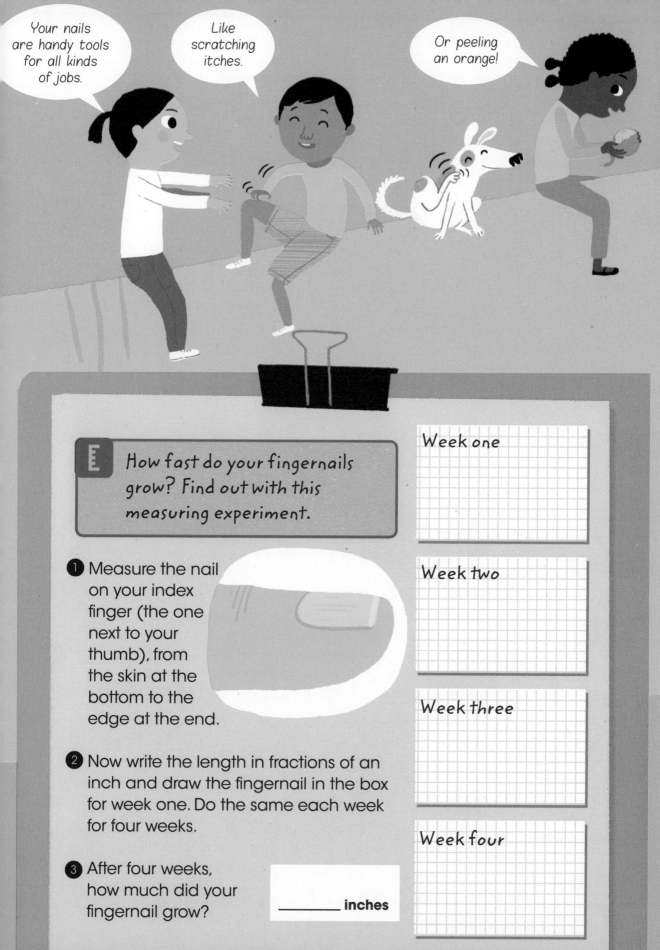

Your nails are handy tools for all kinds of jobs.

Like scratching itches.

Or peeling an orange!

E How fast do your fingernails grow? Find out with this measuring experiment.

1 Measure the nail on your index finger (the one next to your thumb), from the skin at the bottom to the edge at the end.

2 Now write the length in fractions of an inch and draw the fingernail in the box for week one. Do the same each week for four weeks.

3 After four weeks, how much did your fingernail grow?

_____ inches

Week one

Week two

Week three

Week four

Inside a body cell

Cells are the building blocks that make up your body. We are each made from trillions of tiny cells. Each cell has its own job to do, and there are 200 types of cell doing 200 different jobs!

Now let's take a closer look inside just one body cell!

You've discovered many different types of cell on your journey around the body.

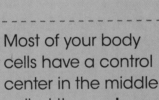

Most of your body cells have a control center in the middle called the **nucleus** (say: new-clee-us).

These shapes are **mitochondria** (say: might-oh-con-dree-aa). They generate most of the energy a cell needs to do its work.

Such as red blood cells, muscle cells, and skin cells!

The outer part of the cell is called the **cell membrane**. This is the cell's skin. It lets water, food, and useful things pass through.

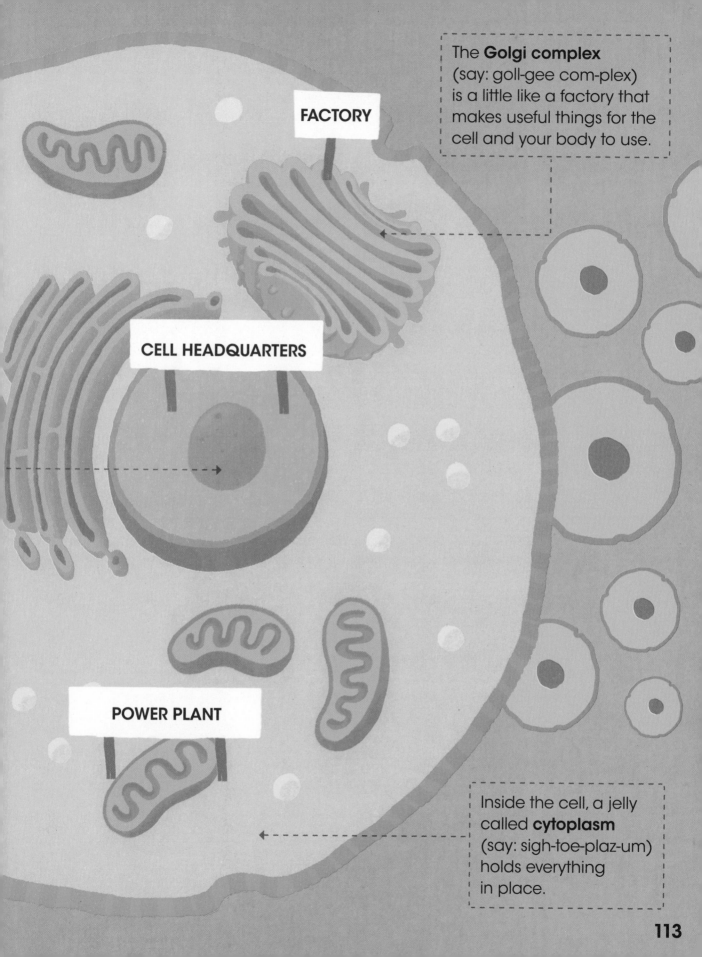

FACTORY

The **Golgi complex** (say: goll-gee com-plex) is a little like a factory that makes useful things for the cell and your body to use.

CELL HEADQUARTERS

POWER PLANT

Inside the cell, a jelly called **cytoplasm** (say: sigh-toe-plaz-um) holds everything in place.

Genius genes

Your body is made of many different types of cell, but how does it know how to make and look after them? The answer lies in your **genes**—a clever secret code, hidden inside your body cells.

Each **chromosome** is made of a long, twisted string of **DNA**.

Inside the **nucleus** of your body cells, there are 46 tiny strands called **chromosomes** (say: crow-mo-sow-mm-s).

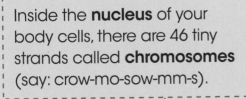

Chromosome

Body cell

Nucleus

The chromosomes sometimes form X shapes. If you're a boy, one of them forms a Y shape.

Every person is different, but human DNA gives us all the same basic body plan. That means that we have the same body proportions. Try this experiment on yourself and a friend.

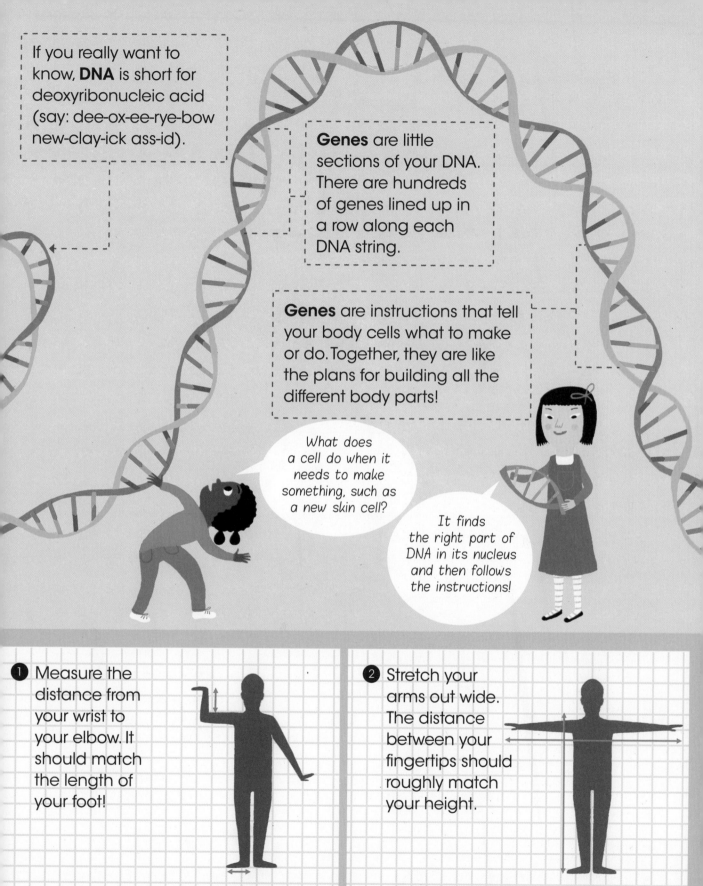

If you really want to know, **DNA** is short for deoxyribonucleic acid (say: dee-ox-ee-rye-bow new-clay-ick ass-id).

Genes are little sections of your DNA. There are hundreds of genes lined up in a row along each DNA string.

Genes are instructions that tell your body cells what to make or do. Together, they are like the plans for building all the different body parts!

What does a cell do when it needs to make something, such as a new skin cell?

It finds the right part of DNA in its nucleus and then follows the instructions!

1 Measure the distance from your wrist to your elbow. It should match the length of your foot!

2 Stretch your arms out wide. The distance between your fingertips should roughly match your height.

DNA roller coaster

If you stretched out all your body's DNA in a long line, it would reach to the sun and back more than three times. Let's take a roller coaster ride on some human DNA!

Each string of **DNA** is actually made of two strands, which are connected like a twisty ladder.

The coded instructions of your **genes** are contained in these links between the strands.

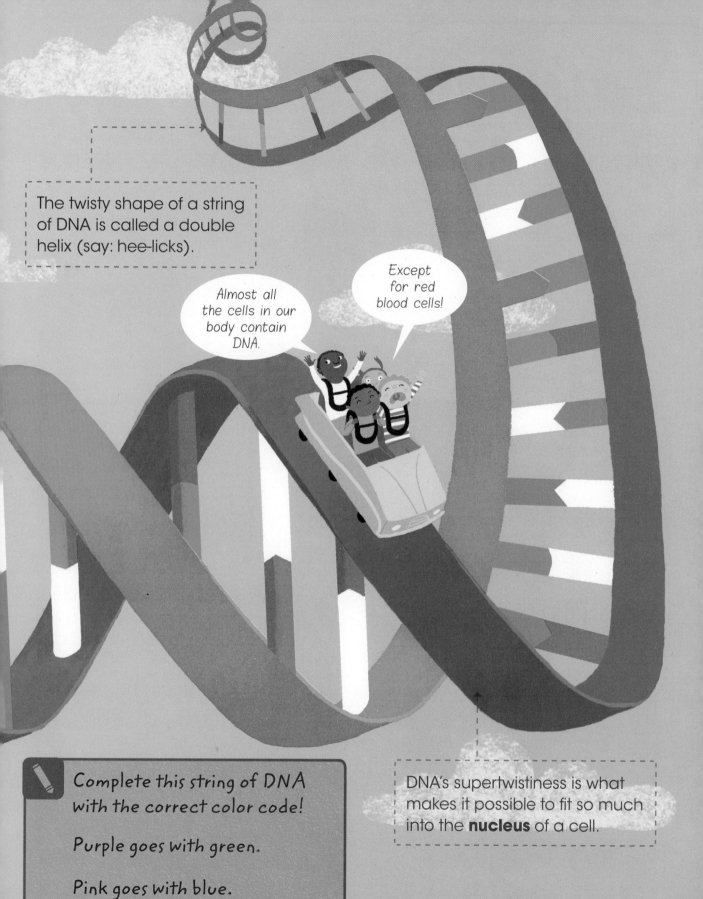

The twisty shape of a string of DNA is called a double helix (say: hee-licks).

Almost all the cells in our body contain DNA.

Except for red blood cells!

Complete this string of DNA with the correct color code!

Purple goes with green.

Pink goes with blue.

DNA's supertwistiness is what makes it possible to fit so much into the **nucleus** of a cell.

Your genes

Genes are what make people look the way they do. They decide many of the things that make you look one of a kind, from head to toe!

Complete the following to reveal how your genes have made you YOU!

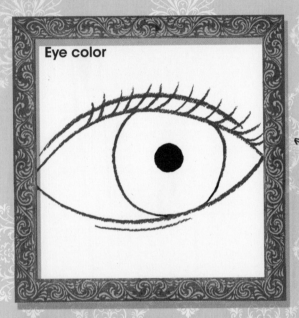
Eye color

Color in your eye and skin color.

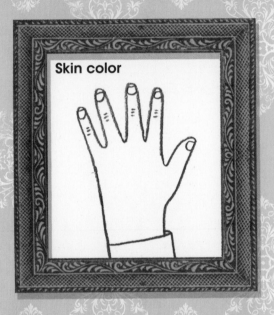
Skin color

Hair color

Scribble in your hair here.

Shape of your ears

Draw in an ear. Either one!

Color in the hand
you write with.

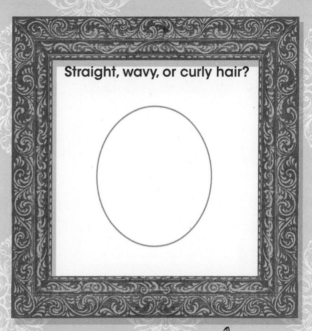

Draw yourself and your
hairstyle in the mirror!

Identical twins look exactly the same
because they share exactly the same genes.
Can you draw in this girl's identical twin?

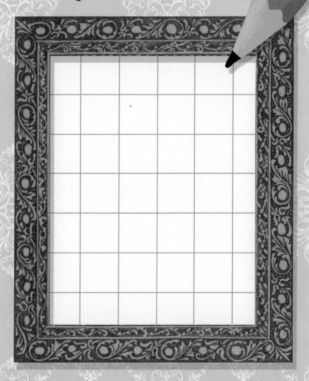

Passing it on

Ever wondered why you've got freckles or curly hair? Well, you can blame your parents, or even your grandparents, for passing them on. It's all down to genes and DNA again!

Babies get a mix of DNA with genes from the cells of the father and the mother.

The way the DNA mixes means that any brothers or sisters get a different mix of genes.

From just one cell with a mix of genes from its parents, a baby grows up to become a totally new person.

That means that you might have your mom's curly hair, while your brother might be tall like your dad!

Grandparents pass on some features to their children, who then pass some on. Mix up some family features to add a girl and a boy to the family tree.

You could give her red hair like her grandma.

You could make him freckly like his dad.

Growing up

Your body is amazing. It starts out as just one cell and ends up as trillions of different cells all working together. Follow the timeline to see how you grow up.

DAY 1
You are just one cell. The cell splits into two and then keeps going.

9 MONTHS
You are a newborn baby. Welcome to the world!

5 YEARS
Your brain is learning a lot. Your milk teeth start falling out to make way for bigger teeth.

10 YEARS
You get much taller. But you're still growing!

Whoa! It all begins with just one tiny cell.

What do you want to be when you grow up? Write a note here to your future self. Remember to check back when you've grown up!

15 YEARS
You get bigger and stronger, and your body changes as you turn into a grown-up.

20 YEARS
Your bones are long, and you have reached your full height. Your body stops growing.

60 YEARS
As you get older, your skin gets wrinkly and your hair gets thinner and turns gray.

To: _____

Date: _____

_____

My plan for when I grow up: _____

_____

_____

Glossary

You can check out the meaning of lots of amazing body words here!

Artery Blood vessel that carries blood away from the heart.

Bacteria Tiny living things that can sometimes cause diseases.

Blood vessel Tube that carries blood around the body.

Capillary Tiny blood vessel that delivers oxygen and food to cells and carries away waste.

Carbohydrate Type of food that gives your body energy.

Carbon dioxide Gas made as a waste product by the body's cells.

Cartilage Tough, rubbery material found in joints and some other parts of the skeleton.

Cells Tiny units that living things are made up of.

Cochlea Snail-shaped part inside the ear.

Diaphragm Muscle under the lungs that pulls down to help you breathe in.

Digest To break down food and soak up the useful parts of it.

Genes Instructions in cells that control the way they work.

Gland Body part that releases a substance, such as sweat or saliva.

Joint Connection between bones.

Kidneys Two organs that filter the blood and remove waste water and chemicals.

Ligament Tough cord that links bones together at a joint.

Minerals Nonliving substances that the body needs, such as calcium.

Muscle Body part that gets shorter and pulls to make the body move.

Nerve Pathway between the brain and body that signals travel along.

Neuron Type of body cell that makes up nerves and the thinking parts of the brain.

Organ A complex body part that does a particular job, such as the brain or lungs.

Oxygen Gas found in the air that body cells need in order to work.

Peristalsis Squeezing action that pushes things along inside tubes in the body.

Pores Openings in the skin that let sweat out.

Protein Type of food that is used to build and repair body parts.

Pulse Your heart rate, or the number of times the heart beats in a minute.

Rectum Tube at the end of the large intestine that carries poo out of the body.

Reflexes Automatic body reactions, such as blinking when something comes near your eyes.

Retina Area of light-sensitive cells inside the back of the eyeball.

Senses Ability to detect different things outside the body, such as seeing, hearing, and smelling.

Skeleton Framework of bones that support the body.

Spinal cord Big bundle of nerves in your back, connecting the brain to the rest of the body.

Sweat Liquid released from the skin to help you cool down.

Taste buds Tiny taste-detecting organs found in the tongue.

Tendon Strong cord connecting a muscle to a bone.

Ureter Tube that carries urine from a kidney to the bladder.

Urine Waste liquid collected by the kidneys.

Vein Blood vessel that carries blood toward the heart.

Vitamins Chemicals found in food that the body needs in small amounts.

X-ray Type of photograph that can show some of the parts inside the body.

I'm using one of my body's senses to read these words.

Index

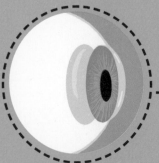

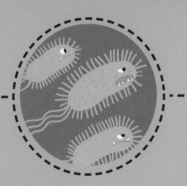

Answers

Page 21

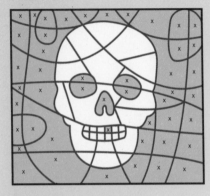

Page 27 25 muscles!

Pages 32–33 Meat—proteins, cheese—fats (but also proteins), orange juice—vitamins and minerals (but also carbohydrates), pasta—carbohydrates.

Page 37 True

Page 39 B

Page 41 Apple

Page 46–47 1. False, 2. False, 3 True, 4. True, 5. True.

Page 49 Wholewheat pasta and vegetables are high in fiber.

Pages 50–51

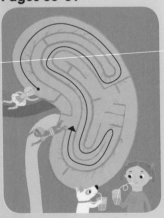

Pages 52–53

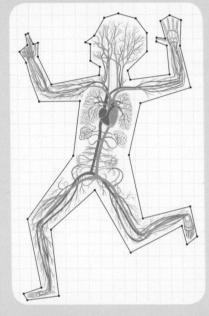

Pages 54–55

Page 57 1. 2. 3.

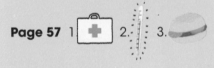

Page 81 A dog.

Pages 82–83 The two blue trees are the same size. The rows of tiles go straight across—it is an illusion. The two dots are the same size.

Pages 90–91 Pain—D, Cold—B, Heat—A, Pressure—C.

Page 99 One possible route is:

Page 105 1. True, 2. False, 3. True.

Page 111 Your fingernails will have grown about a tenth of an inch in one month.

Page 116